THE DEPARTMENTAL GUIDE AND RECORD BOOK FOR STUDENT OUTCOMES ASSESSMENT AND INSTITUTIONAL EFFECTIVENESS

By the same author

Assessment Case Studies: Common Issues in Implementation with Various Approaches to Resolution

A Practitioner's Handbook for Institutional Effectiveness and Outcomes Assessment Implementation

THE DEPARTMENTAL GUIDE AND RECORD BOOK FOR STUDENT OUTCOMES ASSESSMENT AND INSTITUTIONAL EFFECTIVENESS

by **James O. Nichols**

Director, University Planning and Institutional Research, University of Mississippi

AGATHON PRESS
New York

This is a substantially revised and expanded version of
*The Departmental Guide to Implementation of Student Outcomes
Assessment and Institutional Effectiveness,* Agathon Press, 1991

© 1991, 1995 by James O. Nichols

AGATHON PRESS
100 Newfield Avenue
Edison, NJ 08837

Library of Congress Cataloging-in Publication Data
    The departmental guide and record book for student outcomes
assessment and institutional effectiveness / by James O. Nichols
        p.   cm.
    Rev. ed. of: The departmental guide to implementation of student
outcomes   assessment and institutional effectiveness. 1991.
        ISBN 0-87586-114-8
        1. Education, Higher—United States—Evaluation—Handbooks,
manuals, etc. 2. Universities and colleges—United States—
Departments—Evaluation—Handbooks, manuals, etc. 3. Universities and
colleges—United States—Examinations—Handbooks, manuals, etc.
    I. Nichols, James O. (James Oliver), 1941- Departmental guide to
implementation of student outcomes assessment and institutional
effectiveness. II. Title.
    LB2331.63.N52   1995
        378.1'07—dc20   95-44077
                                                                                              CIP

CONTENTS

PREFACE

On any campus there are three entities involved with the implementation of institutional effectiveness or educational (student) outcomes assessment. These entities are: (a) the Chief Executive Officer, (b) the individual or group charged by the Chief Executive Officer with the responsibility for implementation, and (c) the academic and nonacademic departments where implementation will actually take place. Chief Executive Officers can reasonably (given their other responsibilities) be expected to do no more than understand the importance of institutional effectiveness or educational (student) outcomes assessment implementation, give their active support to the process, and provide the resources to see that the job gets done. The individual or group given responsibility for implementation on campus can be expected to organize and support the process. However, the majority of the actual work in implementation of institutional effectiveness or educational (student) outcomes assessment will take place within the institution's academic and nonacademic departments.

A Practitioner's Handbook for Institutional Effectiveness and Student Outcomes Assessment, now in its third, revised and updated edition, is intended to be a working reference for that individual or group on the campus charged by the Chief Executive Officer with responsibility for implementation of institutional effectiveness or educational (student) outcomes assessment. *A Practitioner's Handbook* (3rd ed.) provides a generic model for implementation of institutional effectiveness and educational (student) outcomes assessment as well as resource sections containing detailed information regarding essential components of the implementation process. *Assessment Case Studies* relates the manner in which eleven institutions, relatively mature in the implementation process, dealt with common issues encountered in the process from the institutional to the departmental levels. This second edition of *The Departmental Guide and Record Book,* also revised updated, is designed to assist the busy departmental administrator in leading the implementation process within the individual departments and programs at the institution and recording the results of that implementation. The three publications, *A Practitioner's Handbook* (3rd ed.), *Assessment Case Studies*, and *The Departmental Guide* (2nd ed.), are complementary and cross-referenced for convenience.

The Departmental Guide and Record Book is not meant to be a scholarly work; references are included in only those few instances in which not to do so would border upon plagiarism. It is intended as a document that can be reviewed quickly by the reader who has little time for (or perhaps interest in) assessment theory, but is required to guide implementation within the department. Completely new in this edition is the final section (Appendices A & B), which contains forms that are designed to be photocopied on 8½ x 11 sheets at an enlargement scale of approximately 133%. The forms may then be completed by the department as a record of implementation of institutional effectiveness and/ or assessment of educational outcomes.

Over the last eight years, the author has assisted over 100 institutions from major research universities to two-year colleges in the implementation of institutional effectiveness and educational (student) outcomes assessment activities. During the course of that service, discussions with the departmental chairs have brought forth a relatively consistent series of issues or questions requiring resolution by departmental administrators in the course of implementation. This experience, actually working with departmental administrators implementing institutional effectiveness or assessment of educational (student) outcomes, has formed the basis for the material contained in *The Departmental Guide and Record Book*.

If implementation activities on campus are to be successful, there is no doubt that the Chief Executive Officer must support such action and that the individual or group charged with responsibility for the effort must function effectively. However, equally as important (many would say more important) is the role of the departmental administrator in implementation. Institutional effectiveness and educational (student) outcomes assessment is not possible on a campus without successful implementation within academic and nonacademic departments. *The Departmental Guide and Record Book* is intended to assist those charged with this responsibility.

James O. Nichols
October 1995

The author gratefully acknowledges the support of the University of Mississippi in preparation of this publication.

Chapter 1

WHAT CAN BE EXPECTED FROM *THE DEPARTMENTAL GUIDE AND RECORD BOOK?*

The purpose of *The Departmental Guide and Record Book* is to provide a brief resource to explain and assist in implementation of educational (student) outcomes assessment or support of institutional effectiveness activities within the academic and nonacademic departments of an institution. *The Departmental Guide and Record Book* is unashamedly prescriptive in nature, suggests certain actions, provides a usable format for departmental implementation, and describes departmental implementation as part of an overall institutional program. While most readers of *The Departmental Guide* do not have time to "reinvent the assessment wheel" and hence, the "cookbook" approach offered in this publication, there is no implication that the methodology proposed herein is the only one through which successful implementation can be achieved.

As you review this document, you should make a list of points "for further clarification" or "to challenge" regarding the appropriateness of the procedures suggested for your specific department. The value of *The Departmental Guide* is not in providing a fixed set of activities for departmental implementation, but in offering a "starting place" which will raise many of the issues that must be resolved on each campus and in each department for implementation to successfully proceed. Following resolution of these issues and based upon the guidance contained in the following pages, each department's needs should be relatively self-evident.

How Does *The Departmental Guide and Record Book* Relate to *A Practitioner's Handbook for Institutional Effectiveness and Outcomes Assessment Implementation* (3rd ed.)?

The two publications are closely related. *A Practitioner's Handbook* (3rd ed.) is intended for the institutional level person or group charged by the Chief Executive Officer with coordination of overall institutional effectiveness implementation. Hence, *A Practitioner's Handbook* (3rd ed.) is longer, covers a greater breadth and depth of information providing additional references for clarification, and focuses at a different level (the institutional) than does *The Departmental Guide and Record Book*. Additionally, *A Practitioner's Handbook* (3rd ed.) is premised upon implementation of a comprehensive program of institutional effectiveness operations, which is one of several contexts within which *The Departmental Guide and Record Book* may be found useful.

While compatible with and supportive of *A Practitioner's Handbook, The Departmental Guide and Record Book* is more than a summary of the points made in *A Practitioner's Handbook* (3rd ed.). Though there is naturally a considerable overlap of subjects and examples between the publications, *The Departmental Guide* addresses these subjects from the perspective of a departmental administrator charged with implementation. It seeks to raise and, where appropriate, answers the questions which most departmental administrators pose.

Establishing a Consistent Assessment Terminology

There are enough different terms regarding assessment utilized in various portions of the country to fill several pages. *The Departmental Guide and Record Book* (2nd ed.) as well as *A Practitioner's Handbook* (3rd ed.) and *Assessment Case Studies* attempt to use a consistent set of relatively generic terms to describe activities at the institutional and departmental/program level. The most important of those terms at the departmental level are defined and described below:

- **Intended Educational Outcome**—This term describes *what the departmental faculty intend for a student to be able to think, know, or do when they've completed a given educational program.* In some portions of the country, this is known as an expected educational result, an intended student academic achievement, instructional objective, or intended student outcome. Intended educational outcomes can be assumed to be synonymous with all of these terms for the purpose of this publication.

- **Instructional Departments**—Those entities at an institution in which academic or instructional programs are housed.

- **Educational Support and Administrative Departments**—Those units on the campus that do not house or offer instructional programs and are called upon to establish primarily administrative objectives. There may be some of these units that identify intended research and public service outcomes for the institution; however, the units remain educational support or administrative units in the context described within this publication.

- **Administrative Objectives**—Those statements regarding *what the department intends to accomplish* that are required to be set by educational support and administrative units.

- **Criteria for Program or Departmental Success**—The benchmark that the department sets and against which its performance is judged by the faculty or staff within the department. These criteria are most often stated in terms of percentages, percentiles, averages, or other quantitative measures.

Most of the other terms utilized in this publication are relatively well understood; however, those listed above can cause some confusion due to the use of different terminology in various portions of the country.

Determination of the Context for Implementation and Its Implications for the Department

Very seldom is a departmental administrator asked to implement educational (student) outcomes assessment (or departmental activities to support institutional effectiveness) in a vacuum. Determination of the context or institutional circumstances within which a department is asked to initiate assessment activities is the first priority for a departmental administrator. These contexts can be grouped into the following categories, each of which has its own implications for departmental implementation:

- Implementation of a comprehensive program of institutional effectiveness established to meet regional or other accreditation criteria
- Response to state-mandated assessment programs for accountability to the public
- Assessment of student academic achievement for the purpose of regional or professional accreditation
- Pure/intrinsic student outcomes assessment

A Practitioner's Handbook for Institutional Effectiveness and Outcomes Assessment Implementation (3rd ed.), the publication to which this second edition of *The Departmental Guide and Record Book* is linked, is designed to facilitate implementation of a comprehensive program of institutional effectiveness operations to meet regional accreditation criteria. Figure 1, the Institutional Effectiveness Paradigm shown on the following page, illustrates this context.

In this paradigm, (a) the institution establishes an Expanded Statement of Institutional Purpose; (b) academic and nonacademic departments identify statements of Intended Educational (Instructional or Student), Research, and Public Service Outcomes and Administrative Objectives which are linked to and support this Expanded Statement of Institutional Purpose; (c) assessment of the extent to which departmental and program statements of intended outcomes or objectives are met is accomplished; (d) the results of assessment activities are utilized both to determine the extent to which departmental intentions have been met (hence, effectiveness of the institution has been demonstrated) and to improve departmental and programmatic operations. Within this context (See pages 7 through 11 of the third edition of *A Practitioner's Handbook* for a more detailed description of the Institutional Effectiveness Paradigm), the department will be expected to:

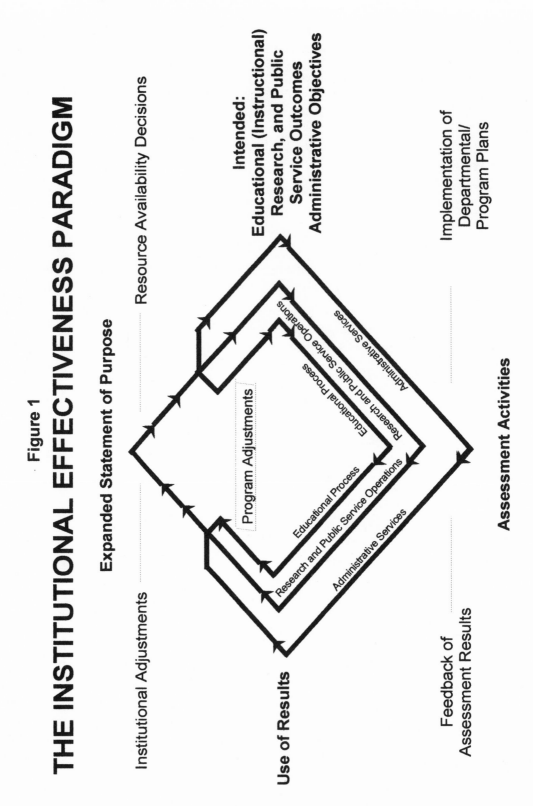

Figure 1

THE INSTITUTIONAL EFFECTIVENESS PARADIGM

- Establish statements of intended educational, research, or public service outcomes or administrative objectives which are related to or supportive of the Expanded Institutional Statement of Purpose;
- Play a major role in identification, and to varying degrees implementation, of procedures and means to assess the extent to which departmental intended outcomes or objectives have been accomplished; and,
- Use the results of assessment to improve student learning or departmental operations.

What are the primary implications for a departmental administrator being asked to implement assessment activities as part of a comprehensive program of institutional effectiveness?

- An institutional statement of purpose exists which the department is being asked to support through establishment of statements of intended educational outcomes or administrative objectives. This statement of institutional purpose is of vital importance in guiding departmental implementation.
- The purpose of departmental implementation is to demonstrate at that level a set of assessment procedures which the campus has relative freedom to develop, rather than to meet externally determined student performance standards.
- Other portions of the institution (including nonacademic departments) will be implementing this process concurrently and common institutional formats and means of assessment may be available to assist the department.
- The department will ultimately need to demonstrate and record its use of assessment data to improve student learning and/or its own operations.

Within this institutional effectiveness context, departmental statements of intended outcomes or objectives and assessment of their accomplishment are the **means** through which institutional effectiveness is validated. Hence, comprehensive implementation ultimately in all academic programs and nonacademic departments is essential and will be required of the institution.

To a departmental administrator, implementation of outcomes assessment as a "response to state-mandated assessment programs for accountability to the public" has a number of substantive implications.

- The purpose of implementation is to impress the public; hence, objectivity is limited, use of the resulting data for improvement of learning is often considered inconsequential, and faculty resistance is assured.
- If institutions are required to submit an assessment plan for approval and then to submit evidence of the plan's implementation, there are a number of decisions which the department needs to consider in design of the plan which will impact its usefulness on the campus.
- The use of standardized cognitive examinations will be either mandated or

strongly suggested by the state as these instruments have more apparent validity with the public and will facilitate comparisons across institutions.

- Implementation in only those departments/programs required by the state is probable, therefore, institutional support and guidance may be limited. However, pressure for impressive assessment results will be maximized.

Implementation of educational (student) outcomes assessment for accountability purposes is the most sterile, potentially prescriptive, threatening, and largely unproductive (as to impact on the institutional operations) context for implementation at the departmental level.

Some regional and professional accrediting associations require that member institutions "assess student academic achievement." This emphasis is apparently less upon demonstration of overall institutional effectiveness through assessment of departmental intended educational outcomes or administrative objectives linked to an institutional statement of purpose than it is on assessment for improvement of student learning. Among the professional as well as regional accrediting associations, there remains the flexibility to identify means of outcome assessment and, in most cases, for the institution to set its own standards for student achievement. In many of the regional and professional accrediting associations who utilize this method, this approach appears to be at least as much focused upon the act of assessment, as on the following actions to improve student learning. What then are the implications for departments implementing assessment of student academic achievement under these conditions?

- Less tie to the institutional level is required.
- A clear understanding of the specific (professional or regional) accreditation criteria will be needed.
- Locally developed, as well as standardized means of assessment, should be considered.
- Even if not required by the accrediting agency, departments should identify intended educational outcomes to focus the assessment effort on their most important expectations and to avoid assessing only those items which are easily measurable, but which may be of little importance.

The most ideal, and least likely, circumstance under which a department will be asked to undertake implementation of educational outcomes assessment activities is that based solely on the intrinsic merit of the process. Under these circumstances, no external pressure is exerted on the institution and motivation for implementation flows from one or more individuals in the institution or potentially the department. The focus of such motivation is probably improvement of student learning. The implications of such implementation include:

- Little pressure, control, or support for the effort beyond the institution and potentially the department.

- Greater likelihood of positive faculty support and involvement.
- Shorter duration of implementation as key individuals change positions.

Each of these contexts (institutional effectiveness, state-mandated accountability, assessment of student achievement for accreditation, and implementation based upon intrinsic value) bring with it a host of implications some of which have been addressed. However, to fully understand the nuances of an individual campus's implementation, the following questions should be raised and answered:

FIGURE 2

Basic Departmental Questions Which Should Be Answered by the Institution

- Why is our department being asked to implement educational outcomes assessment activities (establishment of context)?
- What specifically is expected as a result of the department's efforts and by when?
- What are other components of the institution being asked to accomplish and how should our departmental implementation relate to theirs?
- What coordination, technical expertise, and/or logistical support can the department expect from the institution's central administration?
- Is their a standardized institutional form or format for recording departmental assessment activities?

Is It a Degree Program, Major, Emphasis, or Concentration?

Most regional accrediting agencies require the establishment of statements of intended educational outcomes for academic programs at institutions. The problem is in defining what is an academic program at the institution. At public institutions, the term academic program is normally defined in terms of courses of instruction approved by a central governing board or coordinating agency and most commonly listed in a *degree program inventory* for the institution. In the case of private institutions, an academic program is normally identified as the *majors* which the institution indicates offering in its catalog. The difficulty at both public and private institutions are those groups of courses known as an "emphasis" or "concentration" within a degree program or major. The question becomes when is an "emphasis" or "concentration" an academic program? In many cases in the public sector, truly different courses of instruction have been merged under one degree program umbrella in order to insure their continuation through the maintenance of a sufficient number of graduates to avoid termination by the state agency. It is suggested that in the case of the public sector in particular, the institution begins its definition of an academic program at the degree program level and then (only when apparently needed) examine within the degree programs the nature of the course(s) of instruction actually offered under that designation. If there are substantial differences (defined as 18 unique hours to an area of study at either the graduate or undergraduate level) in the courses of instruction within a single degree program, then in essence there is a separate major or degree program in existence. Under those circumstances, separate sets of intended educational outcomes should be prepared for each of the different courses of instruction within a given degree program. Private colleges may find this approach necessary also. It should be borne in mind that the more different sets of intended educational outcomes established, the more assessment work will be necessary.

Use of *The Departmental Guide and Record Book* in Implementation

Regardless of which context for implementation is identified as being present at an institution, the departments should: (a) identify intended educational, research, and public service outcomes or administrative objectives; (b) develop, and in some cases implement, appropriate assessment procedures to determine accomplishments of their departmental or programmatic expectations identified; and (c) be able to demonstrate use of assessment results to improve student learning or departmental operations. Chapters II and III of this *Departmental Guide* will "walk you through" many of the issues you'll face in this task and suggest common sense solutions gleaned from working with more than 100 institutions as they have implemented outcomes assessment in one context or another. It should be emphasized that there exists a logical order for implementation activities at the departmental level. That order is the **establishment of intended educational outcomes followed by the identification of appropriate means of assessment**. At many colleges, the tendency will be to "jump" to identification of the means of assessment which are tangible entities and then to "backtrack" into identification of the intended educational outcomes which those means of assessment were designed to measure. This action repeatedly results in frustration, useless expenditure of funds, and failure to utilize the results of means of assessment. Readers are urged to follow the activity shown first in Chapter II, regarding identification of intended educational outcomes and then to move to the material in Chapter III, regarding means of assessment. Chapter IV discusses "closing the loop" to demonstrate use of assessment results to improve programming, introduces the complete "five column model," and references the Assessment Record Book contained in Appendix A. Chapter V discusses implementation within educational support and administrative departments. Chapter VI draws together some recurring themes in closing. Take the next few hours (approximately seventy pages) to profit from the experience of others, and ease your own departmental implementation.

PREPARING STATEMENTS OF INTENDED EDUCATIONAL (STUDENT) OUTCOMES

What Are Statements of Intended Educational (Student) Outcomes and Why Need We Prepare Them?

Statements of intended educational (student) outcomes are descriptions of what academic departments intend for students to know (cognitive), think (attitudinal) or do (behavioral) when they have completed their degree programs, as well as their general education or "core" curricula. While some departments such as English and mathematics (due to their heavy service course commitments) will have primary interest in statements of intended educational (student) outcomes established for the general education program, most departmental attention will be focused on development of statements of intended educational outcomes for each degree program (major) in the department.

If the department is implementing assessment activities as a portion of a comprehensive program of institutional effectiveness, it will be required to establish statements of intended educational outcomes linked to and supporting the Expanded Statement of Institutional Purpose. If not, the department should establish such statements for its own use to focus the assessment effort and increase the probability of use of assessment results in a meaningful way by the faculty.

No institution or department has the resources or time to continually assess all possible aspects of each academic program. Given this limitation, priorities for the assessment effort must be set to avoid measuring the meaningless as an easy way out, or "choking to death" on an assessment effort of gargantuan size. Hence, it is logical to begin or focus the department's assessment efforts on those expectations for graduates which have been identified as of primary importance.

In the case of state assessment initiatives for accountability purposes in which even the specific assessment instrument may have been mandated, the primary challenge (other than doing well) will be developing some sense of faculty ownership and willingness to use the resulting data. By bringing forth statements of intended educational (student) outcomes in the cognitive area covered by such mandated assessment procedures, there becomes a limited departmental need for and potential use of results of such state-mandated assessment instruments.

The Nature of Statements of Intended Educational (Student) Outcomes

Results vs. Process

If you ask faculty in most academic departments "What do you do?" the majority will respond, "I teach." If you ask most departmental administrators "What does your department do?" many will respond that the department "teaches classes," "offers programs," or perhaps "conducts research." Each of these responses, while undoubtedly correct, illustrates the extent to which we in academe are focused upon the educational "process" or what we (faculty) intend to do, rather than upon what the impact or result of our actions will be on our students or clients. To use an athletic analogy, we focus on perfecting plays (classes) or a combination of plays (curricula) rather than the final score (the knowledge, attitudes, or abilities our graduates have acquired).

This traditional "process" orientation or focus within academe is frequently reflected in statements of departmental intentions which describe: "adding another course to a major," "reducing teaching loads," "improving faculty development programs," and that all-time favorite, "raising salaries to regional or national averages." As laudable as each of the above notions may be, they do not constitute statements of intended educational or student "outcomes" and should be avoided in the pursuit of institutional effectiveness. It is important to note that the establishment of intended educational (student) outcomes is most related to educational planning, rather than fiscal or resource oriented planning efforts which may be in existence at the institution.

Results-oriented statements of intended educational (student) outcomes should resemble statements describing what graduates or program completers will know (cognitive), think (attitudes), or do (behavioral/performance). In addition to this being a relatively different manner of thought for some in academe, it can be both difficult and threatening. It requires additional thought to extend our planning past what we are doing toward what the impact of this action will be. In other cases, faculty may be unable to identify a desirable intended result of their activity (teaching a particular class), but know that they enjoy teaching that class. In either case, exertion of the necessary additional thought by "screwing up one's courage" to admit that the contribution of some courses to program intended educational outcomes is not apparent must be accomplished so that statements reflecting the most important intended educational outcomes in each program can be formulated.

The Importance (?) of Stating Intended Educational (Student) Outcomes in the Correct Manner

Several times in the history of higher education, waves of behaviorism have threatened to engulf the academic enterprise in an ocean of requirements, methods, criteria, and/or specifications concerning the "correct" method for stating educational objectives in behavioral (outcomes) terms. The rejection of this misplaced emphasis on "means" and "form," coupled with a reluctance to tolerate such "educationese" by the balance of the academic community, has made the mention of (not to even think of discussion and implementation) "student outcomes" an almost blasphemous act in some liberal arts departments.

There is no "correct" means or method for stating intended educational outcomes. The only criteria of paramount importance to consider regarding the means for expressing statements of intended educational outcomes is that the statements are clear and well understood by faculty in the department. In that regard, statements emanating from the faculties in the humanities can be expected to be very different from those of the faculties in business. Those statements from fine arts faculty will be very different from engineering faculty. In all of these cases, each statement can be viewed as correct if it is clearly understood by its originators and is student (results) oriented.

If you, as a departmental administrator, focus on or are provided with a prescriptive set of requirements, specifications, or criteria for wording statements of intended educational outcomes, you can count on a high probability of failure in your implementation effort. Faculty are generally willing to discuss, debate, and work diligently on matters of substance regarding their discipline; but most have little patience with what they perceive as a misplaced emphasis upon bureaucratic procedures.

Virtually the entire effort in identification of intended educational outcomes for each degree program should be directed at the substance of those outcomes, rather than the means for their expression. This focus on substance will be more than a sufficient challenge for most faculties and if there exists an absolutely compelling reason for the standardization of expression, it can be accomplished at the institutional level (with appropriate review by each department).

How Many Statements of Intended Educational (Student) Outcomes Are Necessary for Each Program?

This question is similar to that asked by freshmen regarding their first composition, "How long must it be?" The answer is similar to that allegedly offered by faculty: "Long enough to cover the subject without exhausting the reader." As a guide, it is suggested that between three and five statements of intended educational outcomes be identified for each academic program in the department, though there is nothing magical about these numbers.

Why such a small number of statements? There are both conceptual and pragmatic reasons to limit the number of statements of intended educational outcomes per academic program. From a conceptual standpoint, it is important to recognize that such statements are intended as overarching concepts which should span several courses and are not individual course objectives taken from each syllabus. However, from a practical point of view, there are many other reasons to limit the number of statements of intended educational outcomes being considered at one time.

First among these pragmatic reasons to limit the number of statements of intended educational outcomes is the fact that for every intended educational outcome, there will need to be developed at least one means of assessment to determine its accomplishment. Hence, the identification of intended educational outcomes forms the framework around which the assessment plan must be constructed. If a large number of intended educational outcomes are identified, then a large and elaborate (expensive) assessment mechanism will be necessary.

Who will accomplish this large and elaborate assessment program? The answer is that additional staff (administrators) will need to be employed, thus diminishing the educational focus of the institution, or that the burden will be "dumped" on the already heavily loaded faculty as part of their "professional" responsibility. Either solution is equally wrong and can be avoided with serious discussion among the faculty regarding the "most important" intended educational outcomes at any given time (See further discussion of this subject on page 25).

Second, in most academic programs, there are only a handful (three to five) of intended educational outcomes which the department can emphasize at one time. Departments frequently try to claim that they pursue a number of ends simultaneously; however, when reviewed carefully, there are relatively few common abilities or attitudes which we attempt to instill in our students.

Third, even if otherwise feasible, the establishment of a large number of intended educational outcomes and their necessary assessment procedures would constitute a stack of paper sufficient to "choke the proverbial horse" and little use would be made of the results. Thus, the effort and funds would have been expended only to realize little benefit because of the massiveness of the effort and data generated.

If there ever existed a subject in which the "KISS" (Keep It Simple Stupid) principle applied, outcomes assessment in higher education is that subject. Limiting the number of statements of intended educational (student) outcomes is the first (and many would say most important) step in adhering to that principle. Far better to limit the number of such statements, conduct successful programs of assessment to determine if you are accomplishing these intentions, and use the assessment results to improve student learning, than to curse a large pile of paper which has been difficult to produce, expensive, and is virtually useless.

The Accomplishment of Most Statements of Intended Educational (Student) Outcomes Should Be Ascertainable

The controversy regarding whether the results of what we attempt to accomplish through students is "measurable" has been among the bitterest within and most damaging to higher education. The bitterness has resulted from strongly held positions regarding the nature of our profession and disciplines, and the lack of a clear or common understanding regarding the use of the term "measurable." If academe moves away from a definition of "measurable" which (a) is characterized by a microscope and six-decimal place accuracy, (b) is entirely quantified and precludes qualitative judgments, and (c) is perceived primarily as standardized cognitive examinations, then part of that bitterness will begin to subside. The closer we move to a definition of "measurable" that includes a general judgment of whether students know, think, and can do most of what we intend for them, the easier agreement among faculty becomes. While there are a limited number of intended educational (student) outcomes for which accomplishment will be very difficult to ascertain, this number is surely relatively small.

It is important to get this bitterness behind us because the controversy has upon occasion led faculty to proclaim that since some intended educational outcomes aren't "measurable" (six-digit definition), then all intended educational outcomes aren't "measurable," and that the public should "trust us" and continue to provide funding for our endeavors. Frankly, the public is not buying that position anymore and identifies it as a "cop out." In many states, the requirements for assessment procedures as a form of accountability and reductions in relative funding are clear expressions of public displeasure and loss of confidence in the higher education enterprise

Through agreement upon a number of intended educational (student) outcomes (by far most of which are "measurable"—broad definition) the conduct of appropriate assessment procedures to determine their accomplishment, and the sharing of these accomplishments with the public, a large degree of public confidence in higher education can be restored, and that will serve all types of institutions.

How High Should Intended Educational (Student) Outcomes Be Set?

One of the practical questions departmental administrators will face is posed above. The relatively straightforward answer is to be realistic considering the academic abilities of the students as they enter the program, the level of rigor expected in the classes, and the resources available to support the instructional process.

There is nothing to be gained by setting criteria for intended outcomes (average scores, percentile ranks, etc.) unreasonably high. If an institution operates a virtually open door admissions program, with the result that entering students have diagnostic test scores averaging in the 20–30 percentile range (compared with the national population), there is little chance that its graduates will average in the 80–90 percentile range on most standardized cognitive examinations.

What purpose has been served by setting intended outcomes at that level? The department has looked foolish, the students have been driven beyond reason to attain an unrealistic expectation, and all concerned record a frustrating experience from what may have been a considerable accomplishment (graduation of students who clearly meet or exceed professional standards).

On the other hand, there is also little to be gained from setting intended educational outcomes at such a modest level that any "warm, breathing body" even indirectly exposed to the instructional program can meet them. The educational program at any institution should represent a reasonable challenge for both students and faculty.

It has been the author's experience that most institutions at which "warm breathing body" statements of intended educational (student) outcomes were encountered have been institutions that failed to distinguish these assessment activities from the procedures that exist on all our campuses for evaluation of individual faculty and other employees. It is absolutely imperative that in word, as well as deed, the assessment processes initiated on the campus be held separate from necessary evaluative procedures concerning individuals. Unless this takes place, faculty, being human beings, will insure that they "look good" regarding intended educational outcomes in order to merit increases in rank, salary, or possibly tenure.

In setting criteria for intended educational outcomes, faculty are answering the "ought" question regarding their programming. Having answered the question "What should students be able to think, know, or do?", the "ought" question focuses upon how well should they be able to perform the intended educational or student outcomes identified. The institutions profiled in *Assessment Case Studies* reported almost uniformly that the tendency for the faculty to use assessment results to improve programming was directly linked to the extent to which they identified the criteria for program success (answering the "ought" question) before the actual assessment process took place. When reviewing actual assessment results, if a discrepancy exists between what faculty had previously stated students ought to be able to do (the ideal state) and the actual results reflecting what they can do, faculty will in most cases take the necessary corrective action. However, without such a criterion against which to reflect actual student performance, the tendency to use the data to improve the program is substantially diminished.

At what point in the process should the department establish these criteria for program success, as part of the intended educational (student) outcome or as part of the means of assessment? If in these early stages of identification of the statements of intended educational outcomes faculty become too involved in identification of the answer to the "ought" question and the specific means of assessment to be utilized for measurement, then the focus of the process shifts naturally from student expectations to measurement or assessment. While expression of criteria for program success is certainly possible in the statement of intended educational or student outcomes, "the majority of graduates will be employed upon graduation," in most cases, the identification of this criteria for program success is best selected in conjunction with identification in the means of assessment to be discussed in the next chapter, "50% or more of the students completing the Graduating Student Questionnaire will indicate that they are currently employed or have accepted a job offer at the close of their program."

Preparing Statements of Intended Educational (Student) Outcomes

Role of the Departmental Administrator

The position of the departmental administrator (head, chairperson, etc.) is among the most difficult in higher education and calls for actions ranging from those that can be described as "arbitrary and capricious" to the totally collegial model. In this particular instance, the departmental administrator can assume no more of a leadership role than "first among equals" due to the fact that the issues raised by setting intended educational (student) outcomes are clearly "curricular" in nature, as opposed to "administrative" decisions concerning course scheduling, salary increases, etc. In many ways the departmental administrator's role can be described as that of a "facilitator." Yet those to whom the departmental administrator reports will undoubtedly hold him/her responsible for implementation.

What actions by the departmental administrator are appropriate? Among the actions departmental administrators may undertake to further identification of intended educational outcomes without alienating their colleagues are the following:

- *Gathering information regarding what is expected*—Communication to the departmental faculty of the answers to those questions posed on page 15 is certainly among the duties that can be accomplished.
- *Motivating the faculty to take part*—The single factor reported as the greatest impediment to implementation of educational outcomes assessment is "faculty indifference or resistance." Faculty are frequently indifferent due to a measure of ingrained cynicism, already heavy instructional loads, and resistance based upon allegedly philosophical grounds. The departmental administrator should put the best face on the requirement by seeking to explain the intrinsic value to the departmental faculty of taking part in the activity. Further, integration of credit for participation in the outcomes assessment effort into the departmental and institutional reward structure for faculty will also aid in motivation (See Chapter III of *Assessment Case Studies* for further discussion).
- *Provision of coordination and logistical support*—Establishing the meetings, scheduling the times by which certain decisions should be reached, and providing typing and other services are clearly within the responsibility of the departmental administrator.

- *Getting things moving in a participative, nonconfrontational manner*—Some departmental administrators have found that a useful way to start the discussion regarding intended outcomes is to request that each member of the faculty forward a list of the five most important things which a graduate of each degree program should know or be able to do. From that submission, the departmental administrator can identify those areas in which there is common agreement and focus departmental discussions on refinement of these areas and selection of several others.

It is important that the departmental administrator not force his/her will on the group or appear to do so. Likewise, the statements of intended educational outcomes should not represent the product of several hours behind the departmental administrator's closed door. Unless the faculty feels actively involved in the process of identification of intended educational outcomes, they will not participate in identification of means of assessment, assist in the assessment procedures, or utilize the results of the assessment process.

Role of the Departmental Faculty

The responsibility for faculty control of the curriculum in an institution's degree programs is not challenged by the implementation of educational (student) outcomes assessment activities. Quite the contrary, faculty are requested (or required) to exercise their prerogatives regarding the curriculum, which only they can and should control, perhaps more so than in the past.

As pretentious as the words above may sound, there's some need for such bravado as departmental faculty are asked to address the issue of intended educational outcomes. Not only is the notion of outcomes or results-oriented thinking (as opposed to "process"—see earlier discussion) new and difficult, but discussions focusing on the program as a whole may also be among the first of their kind in the departments. It is not uncommon that strong differences of opinion (which may have been avoided in the past) based on differing points of view concerning the discipline are voiced. In some instances, there exists the danger that faculty will not readily step forward and assume their proper role in identification of intended educational outcomes. In such instances, there is the temptation to "do it for them" in order to meet the departmental deadline. This temptation must be resisted by the departmental administrator, and efforts to involve as many of the faculty as possible in meaningful ways should be redoubled.

Potential Problems in Preparation of Statements of Intended Educational (Student) Outcomes

Faculty Ownership

As just described, motivation of the faculty to take part in identification of intended educational outcomes is likely to be the primary difficulty encountered in implementation. While it is unlikely that all faculty will take part in any departmental endeavor, the offer to take part must be visibly extended on several occasions and the majority of the faculty must play an active role. Endorsement of the effort by the faculty governance structure, in addition to the motivational suggestions mentioned earlier, may help to stimulate participation. Regardless of the means utilized, the statements of intended educational (student) outcomes must be identified closely with the professional judgment of a majority of the faculty in the department.

Limiting the Number of Statements

Once the motivational issue is resolved, the next issue encountered will probably be arriving at a consensus among the departmental faculty regarding the most important three to five statements of intended educational outcomes. Since faculty frequently tend to function in relation to their courses (a portion of a program) and come to naturally believe in the importance of that material in their courses, it is understandable that many faculty will suggest compilation of their course objectives as intended educational outcomes for the academic program. This often results in 30 to 40 or more such statements being suggested among which three to five need to be selected. Review of the statements suggested should identify common themes (bodies of knowledge), abilities, and attitudes that can be discerned among those submitted for consideration. From this review, a number of statements can be drawn, though care will need to be taken not to generalize the description of intended educational outcomes (for the sake of being inclusive) to the point that they loose their identity or sufficient specificity for assessment purposes.

Understanding that consensus will never be completely achieved among the faculty, one means through which to maintain relative harmony among the departmental faculty is to explain the selection of the three to five statements of intended educational outcomes as the "short list" taken from the "long list" of all intended educational outcomes submitted (see Figure 3 on the following page). For practical reasons, the three to five statements selected for the short list are all that the institution and the department can initially afford to establish assessment procedures. Once assessment of these intended educational outcomes is accomplished, some of the statements from the short list may be returned to the long list and statements from the long list moved to the short list for the purpose of initiation of assessment activities. There is no circumstance under which intended educational outcomes for a program need go unchanged for an extended period.

The key to establishing a usable short list of intended educational outcomes is their selection from the long list. If the departmental faculty find that their statements of intended educational outcomes on the short list contain a series of commas, semicolons, or conjunctions, there is a considerable probability that a number of statements from the long list have been combined to establish one intended out-come on the short list. This can work very well where the different items on the longer list speak to the same theme, body of knowledge, or skill. However, in many (most) cases, appearance of these punctuation marks and conjunctions signifies no more than the departmental faculty's desire to be "politically correct" and not to exclude any person from the process. This is particularly the case in smaller departments or those composed of a significant number of untenured faculty members. However, the result of this action is chaos when separate means of assessment must be identified for each of the formerly separate intended educational outcomes specified. At that point, accomplishment of each of the formerly separate intended educational outcomes from the long list will need to be verified (moving the number of assessment activities per academic program from 6–10 to 18–30) and the burden of assessment will become so great as to bog down the process. The key to survival and success in the implementation process at the departmental level is keeping the process simple by faculty selecting the most important intended educational outcomes from the long list.

Figure 3

Short List/Long List Concept

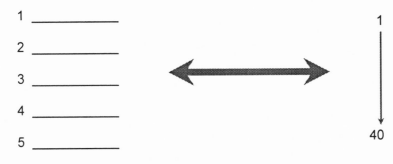

Statements of
Intended Educational Outcomes

Other Valid Statements of
Intended Educational Outcomes

Accomplishment of What Is
Currently Being Assessed

1 _____

2 _____

3 _____

4 _____

5 _____

1

40

Backing into Intended Educational Outcomes from Assessment Means
Human beings imitate one another and educators are certainly no exception. A dangerous problem which may well be encountered is the faculty member who says "the department similar to ours at another college is using the XYZ examination for assessment and I think we should seriously consider its use." The acceptance of a means of assessment utilized by another institution or an available standardized examination indicates that the department has adopted at least the majority of the statements of intended educational outcomes upon which the other institution or test maker has based the means of assessment. While this may be the department's intention, countless departmental faculty have forfeited their prerogatives regarding control of the curriculum by taking this easy way out and unintentionally accepting another group's statements of intended educational outcomes as their own.

Revisions to Statements of Intended Educational (Student) Outcomes

One set of apparent problems, the need to revise statements of intended educational outcomes, will only become evident once means of assessment have been identified. The best statements of intended educational (student) outcomes indicating "appreciation," "understanding," etc., often fade in their attractiveness when faced with the need to identify a means through which to assess or ascertain accomplishment of such lofty ideas. It is quite normal that a number of statements of intended educational outcomes initially established will undergo refinement during identification of the means for assessment of their accomplishment. It is also possible that faced with a lack of ability to identify an appropriate means of assessment, some statements may be moved back to the long list and more assessable statements moved to the short list.

Examples of Statements of Intended Educational (Student) Outcomes

General Comments

On the following pages are four examples (Figures 4-7) of statements of intended educational outcomes, two for four-year institutions and two depicting such statements at two-year colleges. The following general comments relate to all four examples:

Figure 4

Undergraduate English Program

Example of Linkage between Expanded Statement of Institutional Purpose and Departmental/Program Intended Outcomes/Objectives at Our University

Expanded Statement of Institutional Purpose	Departmental/Program Intended Outcomes/Objectives
Mission Statement:	1. Students completing the baccalaureate program in English will compare very favorably in their knowledge of literature with those students completing a similar program nationally.
The principal focus of Our University's curricular program is undergraduate education in the liberal arts and sciences combined with a number of directly career related and preprofessional fields.	
	2. Graduates will be able to critique a brief draft essay, pointing out the grammatical, spelling, and punctuation errors and offering appropriate suggestions for correction of the deficiencies.
Goal Statements:	
Each graduate of Our University will be treated as an individual, and all graduates of baccalaureate-level programs at the University will have developed a depth of understanding in their major field and been afforded the opportunity to prepare for a career or profession following graduation.	3. Students completing the baccalaureate program will be capable of writing an acceptable journal article and having it published.

Figure 5

Accounting Degree Program

Example of Linkage between Expanded Statement of Institutional Purpose and Departmental/Program Intended Outcomes/Objectives at Our University

Expanded Statement of Institutional Purpose	Departmental/Program Intended Outcomes/Objectives
Mission Statement:	1. Students completing the baccalaureate program in accounting will be well prepared for their first position in the field.
The principal focus of Our University's curricular program is undergraduate education in the liberal arts and sciences, combined with a number of directly career related and preprofessional fields.	
	2. Baccalaureate graduates of the accounting program will find ready employment in the field.
Goal Statements:	
All graduates of baccalaureate programs will have developed a depth of understanding in their major field and been afforded the opportunity to prepare for a career following graduation.	3. Graduates will be experienced in the use of microcomputers for accounting procedures.

Figure 6

Your Community College
Transfer Program

Example of Linkage between
Expanded Statement of Institutional Purpose and
Departmental/Program Intended Outcomes/Objectives

**Expanded Statement of
Institutional Purpose**

**Departmental/Program
Intended Outcomes/Objectives**

Mission Statement:

Your Community College is an open-admission, community-based, comprehensive college designed to provide inexpensive, quality educational opportunities (college transfer, career/technical and continuing education) to residents of a five-county service area in the central portion of the Magnolia State.

1. Students transferring will find courses taken at Your Community College fully accepted as the prerequisites for junior and senior level courses at four-year colleges.

Goal Statements:

Serve traditional students seeking the first two years of instruction leading to a bachelor's degree.
a. Recipients of the Associate of Arts (AA) or the Associate of Science (AS) degree will be readily accepted at all public universities in the Magnolia State.
b. Graduates with the AA/AS degree will complete their bachelor's degrees at almost the same rate and in about as much time as students completing their entire degree at four-year institutions in the state.
c. Courses offered at the College as a foundation or prerequisite for courses at four-year colleges will be fully accepted for that purpose.

2. After one year of adjustment to the four-year college, the grades of students transferring from Your Community College will be similar to those of students who initially enrolled at four-year colleges.

3. Students completing the two-year course of study leading toward transfer to a four-year college as a full-time student will complete their baccalaureate degree at almost the same rate as those students originally enrolling at the four-year college.

Figure 7

Your Community College
Automotive Technology Program

Example of Linkage between
Expanded Statement of Institutional Purpose and
Departmental/Program Intended Outcomes/Objectives

**Expanded Statement of
Institutional Purpose**

**Departmental/Program
Intended Outcomes/Objectives**

Mission Statement:

Your Community College is an open-admission, community-based, comprehensive college designed to provide inexpensive, quality educational opportunities (college transfer, career/technical and continuing education) to residents of a five-county service area in the central portion of the Magnolia State.

1. Graduates of the Automotive Technology Program will be successfully employed in the field.

Goal Statements:

Serve persons of all ages in preparing for job entry and careers in a variety of fields.
a. Recipients of an Associate of Applied Science (AAS) degree will be well prepared for first or entry-level positions in a career field.
b. College AAS degree programs will be focused on career-related opportunities for graduates in the five-county area.
c. The majority of AAS graduates will find employment in the five-county area.

2. Graduates of the Automotive Technology Program will be technically proficient.

3. Employers of the Automotive Technology Program graduates in the five-county service area will be pleased with the education received by their employees

a. *Common Format*—While no accrediting agency or, to my knowledge, state agency requires a certain format (form) upon which to record statements of intended educational outcomes, many faculty and departmental administrators are more comfortable if they have a form to complete or common format. The format in which the examples have been presented is one means for expressing the necessary components on one page which clearly shows the relationships between the Expanded Statement of Institutional Purpose, Intended Educational, Research, and Public Service Outcomes and Administrative Objectives. During this publication these examples will be extended to the complete implementation model. However, as useful as this format is to depict the important relationships existing in this process, the feasibility of graphic expression of these components by many departments is not great. Therefore, the Assessment Record Book, described in the appendices to this publication, has been provided to ease departmental record keeping.

b. *Relationship to Expanded Statements of Institutional Purpose*—Each of these examples is linked to the appropriate example Expanded Statements of Institutional Purposes contained in Appendix A, B, or C of *A Practitioner's Handbook* (3rd ed). For institutions implementing educational (student) outcomes assessment at the departmental level within an institutional effectiveness context, this linkage to and support of the institution's purpose is absolutely essential. However, not all departments should expect to support each goal statement within an institution's Expanded Statement of Institutional Purpose. Most academic departments will identify only one (perhaps two) goal statements specifically supported by their academic programs. Departments implementing educational outcomes assessment in other than an institutional effectiveness context may choose to disregard this component of the format.

c. *Simple Wording*—The statements of intended educational outcomes are uniformly simple and straightforward. They are non-technical expressions offered by the faculty in the department regarding what they believe students should know, be able to do, or think upon completion of their programs. In several instances, the general criteria for assessment have been identified within the statements of intended educational outcomes while in others even a general identification has been left for the next phase of the effort—identification of the means of assessment and criteria for success.

Concluding Comments Regarding Identification of Intended Educational (Student) Outcomes

Setting intended educational (student) outcomes for an academic program is a step often overlooked because:

- The department may not be required to identify them.
- Of the threat of "assessment" which dominates the scene.
- Identification of intended educational outcomes can cause disagreements among faculty.

However, on the positive side, setting intended educational (student) outcomes will:

- Establish a positive focus for the assessment effort and reduce its cost.
- Serve a number of constructive uses in curriculum reform outside of outcomes assessment.
- Provide a natural "market" or use for the information resulting from the assessment procedures described in the next chapter.

Once intended educational (student) outcomes are identified for each academic program, the justification for "assessment," and many of the questions surrounding it, will become much clearer and less threatening.

Chapter III

ASSESSMENT OF STUDENT LEARNING

A Means or an End?

Few terms elicit as much anxiety in academe as does the term "assessment." Within the various contexts described earlier, assessment of student learning is considered as both a means and an end. The legislative mandate that certain cognitive tests be administered and the results reported is an example of assessment as an end. This relatively punitive type of requirement serves little purpose and adds further to the negative connotations regarding assessment. On the other hand, when assessment is perceived as a means or bridge between intended educational (student) outcomes and use of the results of assessment to improve instructional programs and student learning, much of the implicit threat of the assessment process is removed. To a greater or lesser degree, all accreditation-based assessment initiatives characterize assessment as a means for improvement of instructional programming. Within this publication the role of assessment as a means is emphasized.

Assessment Is "No Big Deal"

The greatest fear is that of the unknown, and "assessment" is no exception. Among the few guarantees regarding implementation of assessment procedures is that an inventory of current campus practices will reveal several areas (departments, programs, etc.) that already have functional assessment programs in place. These colleagues have been "doing assessment" for their own sake, have not been overwhelmed with the task, and appear to be otherwise relatively normal faculty without particular experience in evaluation methodology.

Assessment activities don't need a rocket scientist to be implemented. They do need careful review of the assessment options (means) available and consideration of the statements of intended educational (student) outcomes and resources available (usually small), as well as the specific requirements placed upon the department. The perfect means of assessment will never exist; however, choices will need to be made and implemented based upon the department's judgment of the best means available at the time. To further compensate for this lack of perfection in means of assessment, it is suggested the several or multiple means of assessment be identified for each intended outcome.

Means of Assessment Available to Academic Departments

Qualitative and Quantitative Means of Assessment
Qualitative means of assessment describe those evaluations in which a holistic judgment concerning a subject is made. Among the best known examples of such qualitative assessment activities are Portfolio Reviews, Public Performances, Oral Examinations, or Dissertation Defenses. In each of these means, there is considerable flexibility on the part of the evaluator, and the assessment takes place within a given context. Such qualitative assessment has a rich tradition (particularly in the fine and performing arts) in higher education; however, it exhibits several limitations:

* *Identification of criteria for success*—Due to the relative subjectivity of most qualitative means of assessment, the identification of specific criteria for assessment and standards for success is difficult.
* *Objectivity of evaluators*—Because those conducting the evaluations are frequently the same faculty who have taught the students during their program, a serious question concerning the objectivity of the evaluators can be raised. This issue may be resolved by the use of external evaluators.
* *Consistency or reliability of judgment*—Assuming that the criteria for assessment can be identified, major problems exist in the consistency with which these necessarily judgmental factors are implemented by different evaluators or from year to year. A solution, though time consuming, is the thorough training of evaluators using identical procedures each year.

Even with the limitations outlined above, qualitative assessment is a legitimate form of assessment which should be seriously considered in any departmental decision regarding the choice of means of assessment.

Quantitative assessment, that form of evaluation characterized by its identification of individual components and provision of quantitative scores, is the form of assessment more commonly implemented. While there are innumerable ways to subdivide quantitative assessment, we have chosen the following three-part taxonomy for ease of discussion: Cognitive Means of Assessment, Assessment of Behavioral Change and Performance, and Attitudinal Assessment. More extensive resource sections regarding each of these subjects are contained in Chapter III of *A Practitioner's Handbook* (3rd ed.) to supplement the following brief discussion of each type of assessment.

Cognitive Means of Assessment
While there are some splendid theoretical arguments concerning the precise meaning of "cognition" in clinical and experimental jargon, the term is used in

assessment circles in relationship to what most faculty would identify as learning or knowledge. This concept of knowledge is differentiated from the students' ability to use knowledge (behavior/performance) and their feeling toward the subject or field (attitudes). Cognitive assessment frequently takes place at the beginning of higher education (placement, diagnostic, or entrance examinations), after completion of the general education component of students' degree programs (rising junior test), and at the conclusion of their course of study (degree program). While some departments, due to their service course orientation, will be concerned about the cognitive assessment of general education, most departmental attention will be focused on cognitive assessment at the close of a student's degree program.

Regretfully, most faculty when thinking of assessment immediately see a student taking a standardized cognitive examination. That is unfortunate, since knowledge is certainly only one component of our intended educational (student) outcomes, and standardized cognitive examinations represent only one type of cognitive assessment. Nonetheless, such instruments are a highly visible form of cognitive assessment.

There are three general types of cognitive standardized examinations commonly utilized in higher education at the end of the students' baccalaureate degree program: professional/graduate school admissions tests, licensure examinations, and standardized achievement tests specifically designed for assessment purposes.

The advantages to utilization of such standardized cognitive examinations include that they are (Ewell, 1987):

- Relatively easy to administer.
- Acceptable in terms of faculty and staff time invested.
- Generally less open to charges of subjectivity or bias by the public (or their representatives).
- Nationally normed for comparisons across institutions.
- Statistically valid and reliable.

However, these instruments exhibit serious disadvantages including that they may (Ewell, 1987):

- Not reflect the department's intended educational (student) outcomes.
- Frequently provide only aggregate scores often not meaningful to assessment of specific intended educational (student) outcomes.
- Compare institutional data to an inappropriate national normative group.
- Be relatively expensive to purchase and score.

As related earlier, the most serious limitation of such standardized cognitive examinations is their potential lack of relation to intended educational (student) outcomes of the program. The first question which must be considered in evaluation of any assessment means is "Does it measure accomplishment of what we intended?" The often negative answer to this question regarding standardized cognitive tests, as well as growing confidence in the institution's own ability to construct comprehensive examinations, are part of the reason that reliance on standardized cognitive measures has declined in recent years (El-Khawas, 1993). Just as the quality and potential usefulness of such instruments has improved, roughly seven out of ten times when faculty review standardized instruments in their field, they are rejected.

Early in the assessment movement, the primary means of standardized cognitive assessment was the achievement portion (subject test) of the Graduate Record Examination (GRE). While this was virtually the only national available standardized cognitive examination at the baccalaureate level, the GRE had been developed for a purpose (screening students for entry to graduate school) unrelated to assessment. While extensive use of these GRE achievement tests as an end of program cognitive assessment was made, its inadequacies for this purpose became quickly apparent.

Several years ago, the Educational Testing Service (ETS) which is the producer of the GRE series began marketing their Major Field Achievement Test (MFAT) developed from the same knowledge (item) base as the GRE, but for assessment purposes. MFAT examinations are available primarily in the same fields as those developed for the GRE as shown below:

Biology	Mathematics
Chemistry	Music
Computer Science	Physics
Economics	Political Science
Education	Psychology
History	Sociology
Literature in English	

These MFAT examinations have proven to be a considerable improvement for assessment purposes over the GRE due to: (a) the availability of specimen copies to compare with departmental intended educational outcomes, (b) score reports in more useful subscales, and (c) more appropriate normative groups. In the summer of 1990, ETS introduced it's first MFAT (Business Administration) developed independently from the GRE. MFAT is a reasonable place to start a department's review of standardized cognitive assessment means should one be available in the field. At the very least, departmental faculty will have the opportunity to review what a national panel of faculty in their discipline has identified as the primary body of knowledge in the field.

In the past, the very limited number of nationally standardized tests available for occupational/technical programs in the two-year college was a significant limitation to assessment of these programs. However, during the last several years the development of the Student Occupational Competency Achievement Test (SOCAT) by the National Occupational Competency Testing Institute (NOCTI) and the Engineering Technician and Technologist Certification Programs conducted by the National Institute for Certification in Engineering Technologies (NICET) has contributed substantially to filling this void. The SOCAT tests cover a wide variety of fields, from child care through horticulture to electronics, and consist of both a written objective test and performance test that are institutionally administered. The NICET certification examinations are available in a much narrower set of fields directly related to the engineering technologies. These NICET examinations also consist of written cognitive examination as well as practical performance tests but are only administered at state testing locations several times each year.

In addition to the MFAT, four-year college departmental faculty should consider both professional school admissions tests and licensure examinations as a means of standardized cognitive assessment, if for no other reason than the fact that many of their students already take such examinations. Professional schools admissions test are an apparent source of assessment data; however, they suffer from two specific limitations. While parts of some such examinations such as the Medical School Admissions Test do measure knowledge, others such as the Graduate Management Aptitude Test (GMAT), the Law School Admission Test (LSAT), and the Dental Aptitude Test (DAT) measure aptitude or general intelligence far more than achievement. Second, because these test are designed for screening purposes, they are highly secure instruments which the faculty will not have an opportunity to review in detail and will receive only highly aggregated results.

Licensure examinations taken by students prior to entry into a profession (Bar, Medical, Nursing, Teaching, Certified Public Accountant, etc.) represent a potentially very useful type of cognitive assessment in the major. Most such licensure examinations vary somewhat by state in either content and/or the amount of institutional feedback of results available. Ideally, their content should relate closely with the intended educational outcomes of the degree programs preparing students for these professions. Where available, the results of such licensure constitute "instant assessment data" for those institutions implementing under the pressure of time.

While the standardized cognitive means of assessment outlined have improved substantially in recent years (as indicated earlier), the clear trend among institutions is toward a more locally developed end of program cognitive measures (El-Khawas, 1993). Among the advantages of construction of locally developed cognitive examinations are the following (Ewell, 1987):

   a. *Reflection of the specific intended educational (student) outcomes identified by the department*—Because of its local development, the examination can be designed to exactly match the intended educational outcomes of the department.

b. *Ability to conduct detailed analysis*—Since the results are available in their entirety, they can be carefully analyzed to determine areas of the curriculum which are supporting accomplishment of intended educational outcomes and those which are not.

c. *Flexibility in format*—Because the examination will be locally scored, a combination of essay, multiple choice, and other type items may be utilized.

d. *Faculty ownership*—Based upon their heavy involvement in all aspects of preparation and grading, departmental faculty have no question regarding the legitimacy of the examination or their ownership and tend to use the results of such examinations more readily.

Despite the impressive advantages cited above, there are numerous disadvantages to the construction and utilization of locally developed cognitive means of assessment. Among these are (Ewell, 1987):

a. *Lack of external credibility*—If the department is implementing in response to a state accountability mandate, there is little likelihood that locally developed instruments will be acceptable. Within accreditation related contexts for implementation, locally developed instruments are usually acceptable.

b. *Lack of comparative data*—The inability to compare student achievements with other institutions limits the nature of statements of intended educational outcomes.

c. *High faculty effort to develop, administer and maintain*—The greatest disadvantage of this approach is the exceedingly great amount of effort needed to develop and maintain such locally developed instruments over a long period of time. While relatively short bursts of faculty energy may be harnessed to develop such tests, most departmental faculty are simply unwilling (in the face of their other duties) to commit high levels of effort to this process over an extended period.

The experience of the case studies institutions in the matter of locally developed comprehensive examinations was disappointing. Fewer such examinations than expected were reported as being implemented by faculty and departments at these eleven institutions. The primary reason most often cited for failure to develop such tests was the lack of release time for development of such instruments. This lack of release time is in agreement with such policies that exist at most institutions nationally and is obviously a primary impediment to the use of locally developed comprehensive examinations. It is the author's opinion that given the amount of work inherent therein, the effort bearing directly upon development of comprehensive locally developed assessment means should be recognized in some way. This recognition may take the form of summer employment, institutionally identified release time, or informal reduction of a faculty member's teaching load by the department chair during the time the test is being prepared. Once the comprehensive locally developed examination is prepared, then, in the author's opinion, administration, grading, and maintenance should be accomplished as part of a normal faculty load without extra recognition or compensation.

While cognitive assessment is clearly only one form of ascertaining accomplishment of intended student outcomes, it is without much question the dominant form. Students attend our institutions primarily to learn or acquire knowledge. Cognitive assessment validates their accomplishment of that purpose. For a more technical discussion of specific standardized cognitive examinations and the sources from which they can be obtained, see the Resource Section, "Cognitive Assessment Instruments: Availability and Utilization" by Krotseng and Pike in the 3rd edition of *A Practitioner's Handbook*.

Assessment of Behavioral Change and Performance
Just as cognitive assessment is the most commonly identified form of assessment, assessment of changes in student behavior and performance is probably the most overlooked form of assessment. This form of assessment relates to what a student *does* or *can do* as a result of accomplishing previously identified statements of intended educational (student) outcomes and is composed of the slightly differing concepts of behavior and performance.

In behavioral assessment one observes what a student does following a given treatment (completion of a degree program) and compares that behavior with the intended educational (student) outcomes of the program. This observation is made concerning an event in the student's life which is not regulated, contrived, or designed for the purposes of assessment.

Examples of such diverse behavioral assessment activities include: employment, admission to graduate school, church attendance, and voting. Many of our degree programs are primarily oriented toward preparation of individuals for employment. Thus the primary criteria for success of the program becomes "Did the graduate find employment in the field?", a matter ascertained by observing the behavior (getting a job) of the graduate upon completion of the program. Likewise, many programs are focused principally on preparation of students for graduate work. The success of such programs may be primarily gauged by the acceptance of baccalaureate graduates into graduate school. The primary purpose of the transfer program of two-year colleges is to prepare students for successful transfer to a four-year college. Without observation of graduate performance at four-year colleges, the two-year college transfer program's success is difficult to ascertain or gauge.

Activities reported by alumni some time after graduation, reflecting attitudes or values that were intended educational (student) outcomes of their program are among the most powerful forms of behavioral assessment. To the Bible college whose students are required to enroll in 30 or more hours of courses related to religion, there is little more gratifying or relevant than responses to an alumni survey indicating a regular pattern of church attendance and leadership by its former students. To the English department faculty who have identified "development of a lifelong love of reading" as an intended educational outcome of their program in Literature, what more satisfying result than alumni who report owning small libraries in their homes, reading several works of fiction each month, or teaching others to read. While observation or reporting of events in the lives of students or graduates is not easily accomplished, it can provide some of the best assessment results received by faculty.

Performance type assessment is similar to behavioral assessment in that it seeks to observe what the student does; however, in this instance, the student is asked to "perform" as a matter of assessment. Few consumers are concerned with the amount of theory that graduates of an associate degree program in Automotive Technology have acquired. They want to know "Can they fix my car?"; hence, such programs tend to identify relatively pragmatic statements of intended educational outcomes, and performance type assessment mechanisms such as that described in the example on page 51. Likewise, while knowledge of medicine is an important requisite for surgeons, it is their ability to perform successful surgery that is assessed during their internship/residency.

The advantages of behavioral or performance assessment relate to:

- Their ability to provide evidence directly bearing on some of the most important intended educational outcomes.
- In the case of behavior, the lack of intrusiveness or very limited amount of additional effort on the part of the graduate to provide the information needed, and the ability to extend such assessment activities to ascertain accomplishment of longer term intended educational outcomes.
- In the case of performance, the opportunity to control external variables to place the students in exactly the surroundings in which the intended educational outcomes should be demonstrated in their professional lives.

The principal disadvantages of behavioral and performance related assessment are:

- Limited applicability of the approach to some academic disciplines.
- Need to receive necessary information from alumni and other institutions (transfer institutions for two-year college students and graduate level institutions for four-year college students).
- Cost of preparation and maintenance of performance tests (particularly over an extended period of time).

- Considerable amount of time necessary to train assessors of student performance to insure reliability.

Due to their nature, few standardized performance means of assessment are available, leaving most to be developed locally. Likewise, much behavioral observation information is gained from local sources or developed instruments.

One type of performance assessment that overlaps with qualitative means and appears at the outset to be particularly attractive (some might even say seductive) is portfolio assessment. In portfolio assessment the performance of students is reviewed based upon a longitudinal collection of their work made during their matriculation at the institution. In the author's opinion, while this is a valid means of assessment, in some aspects of the institution (particularly fine and performing arts and potentially English), it is more often abused than utilized correctly. Its abuse stems from the fact that faculty often see the collection of student class materials as a "quick and dirty" way to begin the assessment process and only when challenged with analysis of the portfolios, does the difficulty of the procedure become evident. Should the faculty desire to utilize portfolio assessment, it is recommended that the specific items from each class to be included in the portfolio be identified beforehand as well as the "quality" that should be demonstrated in each of these items in the portfolio. For additional information on performance assessment, see the resource section "Assessment of Behavioral Change and Performance" by Kinnick and Walleri in *A Practitioner's Handbook* (3rd ed.).

Attitudinal Assessment
It is impossible for faculty to provide all the knowledge and skills which students will need during their lifetime; however, the development of attitudes toward the discipline and the department's relative effectiveness in preparation of its graduates for life beyond the institution will undoubtedly occur. Thus, one form of intended educational outcome frequently identified by departmental faculty relates to the attitudes of students, graduates, alumni, and employers.

The identification of attitudes of students as they enter institutions and subsequently degree programs is frequently accomplished to determine their opinions regarding social, ethical, and moral issues. Such surveys may be utilized as benchmarks with which to compare similar responses after the students completion of the institution's general education or degree programs.

Determination of the students attitudes concerning their discipline, course of study, or the educational support services provided by the institution is often sought at the point at which students leave the institution. This inquiry takes the form of a "graduating student" or "exiting student" (dropout) survey. This survey can be conducted either by written questionnaire or structured interview. The interview approach provides considerable flexibility to pursue particularly strong feelings on the part of individual students. The interviewers utilized by the institution should be carefully trained, nonthreatening, and unbiased.

Alumni surveys are among the most common forms of attitudinal assessment. They provide insight into the long-term development of students and valuable feedback concerning their behavior (employment, further schooling, etc.) after they leave the institution. Such data are frequently handicapped by the difficulty in identifying current attitudes of an unbiased sample of alumni and the fact that the responses of alumni may be to events, programs, and procedures long changed at the institution.

Frequently forgotten in discussions of attitudinal surveys is the determination of employer attitudes toward graduates. While there is a wide divergence of opinion between faculty, administrators, members of governing boards, and the public regarding what constitutes the characteristics of a quality institution, all such constituencies agree that the opinion of employers regarding the ability of institutional graduates is among the most important means through which to identify such an institution.

Attitudinal questionnaires designed for entering students, graduating students, alumni, etc. can be obtained from commercial sources or developed locally. American College Testing, Educational Testing Service, the College Board, and others provide relatively similar products that have been carefully developed, provide normative data with which to compare responses, and offer opportunities for the addition of locally developed items. Unfortunately, these instruments are relatively expensive per unit and offer little institutional identity. Locally developed attitudinal questionnaires can be customized to exactly match statements of intended educational outcomes (and administrative objectives in nonacademic departments), and exhibit a high level of institutional identification (colors, signatures, symbols, etc.) at a relatively low per-unit cost. However, locally developed instruments lack comparability of data and take a considerable amount of time and money to develop. Both commercial and locally developed questionnaires may be utilized to measure change in attitudes as well as attitudes at the end of programs.

Who should develop, support, and implement attitudinal assessment? The answer is clearly not the individual academic or administrative departments. If individual academic and administrative departments prepare their own attitudinal questionnaires:

- The considerable cost (time) needed for local development will be multiplied many fold.
- Students will be bombarded by questionnaires from their academic department, the library, the registrar, etc., and the response rate to all questionnaires will plummet.
- High-priced faculty will become heavily engaged in paper shuffling.
- Computer support will probably not be available for the multiple different formats for questionnaires surely to result.

While individual academic departments should have considerable input into the selection and/or the design of questionnaires to be utilized, and the opportunity to offer items specifically related to their degree program, they should not become involved with the logistics of distribution, processing, and analysis of attitudinal questionnaires. Their role is as one of the primary consumers of the information generated by attitudinal assessment. The central administration at the institution should provide survey research support. Through this mechanism, better surveys at a lower cost per unit are available throughout the institution.

The primary advantage of attitudinal assessment is that it can reflect the feelings and emotions of respondents as no other form of assessment is capable. The primary disadvantages are its considerable cost and the danger that respondents will provide only expected or socially acceptable answers.

Additional information concerning specific standardized attitudinal surveys and guidance for institutional level development of local instruments is continued in the Resource Section "Attitudinal Surveys in Institutional Effectiveness" by Raines, Bridger, and Wolff in *A Practitioner's Handbook* (3rd ed.).

The Nature of the Assessment Process

Who/What Is Being Assessed?

Among the most frequent misunderstandings regarding assessment is its focus or intent. Because on many occasions we must rely upon information originating from students or graduates, it is easy to assume that individual students or graduates are the focus of the assessment effort. In reality, aggregated accomplishments by students of intended educational outcomes is the primary available reflection of our programs and their results, which are the focus of the assessment effort.

What are the implications of understanding this critical difference in perspective?

- Not all students or graduates need take or respond to all means of assessment since a representative sample is sufficient for evaluation of the program.
- Criteria for intended educational (student) outcomes can be stated in terms of a portion of program graduates (as opposed to all) meeting an ambitious criteria.
- Assessment results reflect the accomplishments of the departmental faculty as a whole.

Having stated that the focus of assessment within the context described previously is the department's programs, it must also be indicated that departments may decide to share that focus with their students by requiring before graduation that students take a cognitive comprehensive examinations and achieve a minimum score, or pass a performance test. However, few departments have demonstrated sufficient confidence in their programmatic means of assessment to set other than minimal required levels of achievement by students prior to graduation from the institution. Sharing of the assessment focus with individual students by requiring a minimal score prior to issuance of a degree is practiced by very few institutions and is not recommended by this author.

How Will Assessment Results Be Utilized?

The use of assessment results will certainly vary depending upon the context for implementation identified. If assessment is being implemented as an accountability mechanism in response to a state mandate, the primary use will be external to the institution to satisfy requirements and build public confidence; however, use within the department should also be encouraged. In any of the other context for assessment (institutional effectiveness, assessment of student achievement, or intrinsic motivation), the major use of assessment results will be internal to the institution for program improvement. Additionally, assessment results within the context of institutional effectiveness are utilized also (through intended educational outcomes linked to the institutional level) to validate the accomplishment of the institution's Expanded Statement of Institutional Purpose.

Use of assessment results in relation to individual faculty and students presents some pitfalls and opportunities. Because the focus of the assessment effort is on programs, it is both inappropriate and difficult to attempt to fix responsibility (particularly for shortcomings) on an individual faculty member. If the departmental faculty suspect that assessment is being conducted for personnel evaluation purposes, resistance will grow rapidly, vital participation in identifying intended educational outcomes will substantially diminish, any criteria set for assessment results will be extremely modest, results of assessment activities will be either challenged or unused, and the process will be perceived as a punitive administrative exercise. There is little that can "poison the well" more quickly than a few drops of evidence to support the latent paranoia regarding assessment that one finds on many campuses. To preclude potential misuse or misunderstandings regarding the use of assessment data, some campuses have found it particularly useful to establish a policy statement excluding the use of assessment results for personnel evaluation and approved by the Chief Executive Officer before implementation begins.

Use of assessment results regarding individual students has substantive implications for their motivation. If students are required to accomplish certain levels of achievement prior to being granted a degree (an unusual occurrence), student motivation is assured. On the other hand, if students are required only to "take" or "respond" to assessment measures without a minimum score requirement, or are asked to voluntarily take part in assessment activities, motivational problems will be quickly evidenced. Students must be convinced to take assessment seriously. Among the things that departmental faculty can do to encourage a sincere effort by students are the following:

• Imbed the means of assessment in classes using it once for grading purposes and a second time by the overall departmental faculty for assessment.

- Have faculty members acting as student advisors directly express the extent to which assessment, and the student's role in it, is taken seriously by the department.
- Indicate that assessment results will be among the first items reviewed when providing references to graduate school and for jobs.
- Appeal to the student's sense of interest in the discipline and the welfare of students who will follow them.

Through one means or another, sincere participation by students in assessment activities must be assured. The use of assessment results can be a powerful positive or negative motivator among students and faculty. The case study institutions found imbedding means of assessment in Capstone or other classes near the end of the program to be the most effective means of student motivation (see Chapter IV, *Assessment Case Studies*).

What Role Do Class Grades Play in Assessment?

In most instances, assessment requirements call for assessment beyond the course level. This requirement emphasizes (a) integration of the students' learning experiences across courses in their degree programs rather than from one course and (b) freeing the single faculty member (but not the combined departmental faculty) of the complete responsibility for assessment of program accomplishment through awarding of a grade. Like it or not, public confidence in collegiate grading practices in individual courses is not exceptionally high. Employers have hired too many graduates who, though receiving passing marks and a degree from an institution, do not measure up to expectations.

There are two occasions in which course grades are acceptable as means of assessment. The first of these occasions is utilization of course grades in mainstream courses as a measure of the success of developmental or remedial education. In this case, students have moved from pre-college to college and crossed over into the next level of education. Likewise, grades or grade point averages of students transferring from two- to four-year institutions may be utilized as a means of assessment for the success of the transfer program at the two-year institution. As in the case of developmental education, these students also have moved to the next level of education beyond that which is being assessed.

The inability to utilize grades as a means of assessment is often questioned by faculty. One means to soften this injunction is through explanation of the Column and Row matrix shown in Figure 8. As faculty members, we have in mind certain criteria upon which we base grades and that we expect students to meet in their matriculation through our program and classes. These criteria are identified by the lower case a, b, c, and d in the rows of the matrix shown as Figure 8. As faculty, we're used to the idea of looking down the column in this matrix and awarding the student a grade at the foot of the column as signified by A, B, C, etc. The different columns in the matrix, numbered I-V and beyond, identify

Figure 8

Column and Row Explanation of Relationship Between Individual Student Grading and Educational Outcomes Assessment

Intended Educational Outcomes / Grading Criteria 1-5 Scale	Individual Students Graded by Various Faculty					Criteria/Intended Educational Outcomes Average
	I	II	III	IV	V	
Criteria a	3	4	1	2	3	2.6
Criteria b	2	5	3	2	5	3.4
Criteria c	4	5	2	3	4	3.6
Criteria d	4	3	4	5	3	3.8
Total	13	17	10	12	15	
Individual Student Grade	C	A	D	C	B	

→ Total "Down the Columns" for Individual Student Grading

--→ Analyze "Across the Rows" for Assessment of Intended Educational Outcomes Accomplishment individual students whose collective results in each row of the matrix represent how well students overall passing through the curriculum did in relationship to the different criteria that we as faculty have already established. Thus the data for assessment purposes should be analyzed across the rows in the matrix to determine the extent to which the students are meeting the criteria otherwise known as intended educational (student) outcomes that have been established. In many cases, groups of faculty need only state their existing criteria in terms of intended educational (student) outcomes and reanalyze already existing data across the rows of the matrix (rather than down the columns for individual student grading purposes) in order to have readily usable assessment data available regarding their curriculum in a short time.

Importance of Multiple Measures

Descriptions of the assessment craft as imperfect or being in its infancy remain among the greatest understatements made. Not only are such statements correct, but the appropriateness of many instruments remains to be demonstrated in each institutional context. Not only is the MFAT in English Literature a relatively new instrument, but its suitability for assessment of the intended educational (student) outcomes identified by the English department at a given institution has yet to be demonstrated.

To compensate for the relative immaturity of many of the means of assessment available, several means of assessment should be identified for each intended educational (student) outcome.

By so doing, the results from each means may be compared as a measure of reliability of judgment and a backup will exist should one means prove totally unsatisfactory in practice.

Roles of the Faculty and Administration in Assessment

While the faculty have an important role to play in assessment, it is not as dominant as in identification of intended educational (student) outcomes. Among the appropriate faculty roles are:

- Participation in selection of the best means of assessment available to evaluate the accomplishment of their intended educational outcomes.
- Development, administration, grading, reporting of results, and maintenance of locally developed cognitive end of program examinations.
- Use of results to improve academic programs.

All of these roles describe departmental faculty who are interested in the selection of the appropriate means of assessment; may be responsible for design, administration, and evaluation of locally developed cognitive instruments; are among the primary consumers of information resulting from assessment activities; but who are not responsible for seeing that assessment takes place institution wide.

The primary responsibility for seeing that assessment activities take place should reside with the institution's administration in conjunction with an institutionally based faculty assessment committee in an oversight role. This administrative responsibility for seeing that assessment takes place is premised upon: (a) the need for a limited amount of additional funding for assessment initiatives, (b) the fact that many assessment activities can be more efficiently and effectively conducted at the institutional level, and (c) the already overburdened nature of most departmental faculty. Among the roles which departmental faculty should expect to see being played by central administration are the following:

- *Coordination of assessment activities under the oversight of a faculty committee*—The coordination, avoidance of duplication of effort, and design (if necessary) of common formats for expression of intended educational (student) outcomes and assessment results should flow from the central administration.

- *Provision of technical guidance*—Most academic departments cannot be expected to have technical expertise regarding test construction or survey research. Nor should individual departmental faculties be expected to stay abreast of the development of standardized means of assessment.

- *Logistical support*—The distribution and processing of questionnaires, administration of standardized examinations, and many other assessment measures are primarily clerical in nature. Given the already substantial loads carried by departmental faculty and the nature of the work, the provision of centralized logistical support makes both common and campus political sense.

There is a fine line between coordination/support of and control of any process; however, that is precisely the line that must not be crossed by the central administration. Responsibility for the substantive or policy aspects of the assessment process should be shared by departmental faculty, central administration, and an institutional level faculty oversight committee. The central administration's role should be perceived as coordination and support of activities commonly agreed upon.

Examples of the Use of Various Means of Assessment

Figures 9-12 on the following pages extend the English, Accounting, Auto Technology, and Transfer Examples provided earlier in Figures 4-7 (pages 28-29) into three-column models by identifying specific means of assessment and criteria for program success of each of the intended educational outcomes.

Several things should be pointed out concerning the following examples:

- Note the linkage from the Expanded Statement of Institutional Purpose through Goals, Intended Educational Outcomes, to Means of Assessment and Criteria. The linkage between these components enables the institution to trace the accomplishment of its stated purpose.

Figure 9

Undergraduate English Program

Example of Linkage between Expanded Statement of Institutional Purpose, Departmental/Program Intended Outcomes/Objectives, and Assessment Criteria at Our University

Expanded Statement of Institutional Purpose

Mission Statement:

The principal focus of Our University's curricular program is undergraduate education in the liberal arts and sciences combined with a number of directly career related and preprofessional fields.

Goal Statements:

Each graduate of Our University will be treated as an individual, and all graduates of baccalaureate-level programs at the University will have developed a depth of understanding in their major field and been afforded the opportunity to prepare for a career or profession following graduation.

Departmental/Program Intended Outcomes/Objectives

1. Students completing the baccalaureate program in English will compare very favorably in their knowledge of literature with those students completing a similar program nationally.

2. Graduates will be able to critique a brief draft essay, pointing out the grammatical, spelling, and punctuation errors and offering appropriate suggestions for correction of the deficiencies.

3. Students completing the baccalaureate program will be capable of writing an acceptable journal article and having it published.

Assessment Criteria & Procedures

1a. The average score of the graduates of the baccalaureate program in English on the "Literature in English" MFAT subject test (which they will be required to take shortly before graduation) will be at or near the 50th percentile compared to national results.

1b. Ninety percent of the English baccalaureate program will "agree" or "strongly agree" with the statement "In the field of literature I feel as well prepared as the majority of individuals nationwide who have completed a similar degree during the past year."

2a. As part of a "capstone course" during the students' final semester prior to graduation, they will critique a short draft essay; identify grammatical, spelling, and punctuation errors; and offer suggestions for correction of the deficiencies. Eighty percent of the program's graduates will identify and offer appropriate suggestions for remediation of 90% of the errors in the draft essay.

3a. All graduates of the baccalaureate level program in English will prepare a journal article for submission and forward it to the English department.

3b. Eighty percent of those journal articles submitted will be judged acceptable for publication by a jury of English department faculty from an institution comparable to Our University.

3c. Twenty percent of those articles submitted will be published in student or other publications.

Figure 10

Accounting Degree Program

Example of Linkage between Expanded Statement of Institutional Purpose, Departmental/Program Intended Outcomes/Objectives, Assessment Criteria at Our University

Expanded Statement of Institutional Purpose

Mission Statement:

The principal focus of Our University's curricular program is undergraduate education in the liberal arts and sciences, combined with a number of directly career related and preprofessional fields.

Goal Statements:

All graduates of baccalaureate programs will have developed a depth of understanding in their major field and been afforded the opportunity to prepare for a career following graduation.

Departmental/Program Intended Outcomes/Objectives

1. Students completing the baccalaureate program in accounting will be well prepared for their first position in the field.

2. Baccalaureate graduates of the accounting program will find ready employment in the field.

3. Graduates will be experienced in the use of microcomputers for accounting procedures.

Assessment Criteria & Procedures

1a. Eighty percent of those taking the CPA exam each year and indicating an accounting degree from Our University will pass three of four parts on the exam.

1b. Eighty-five percent of the graduates of the accounting baccalaureate program will "agree" or "strongly agree" with the statement "I am well prepared for my first position" contained in Our University's Graduating Student Questionnaire.

1c. Employers of accounting program graduates hired through the Our University Placement Service will indicate on a survey forwarded to them by the Placement Service one year after employment of the graduate, an average rating of 7.5 or more (on a scale of 1-10) in response to the question "How well was your employee prepared for his position by Our University?"

2a. Ninety percent of accounting graduates registered with the placement service each fall will have received a job offer by the close of spring semester each year.

2b. Sixty percent of students completing the accounting degree program will indicate that they are currently employed or have accepted a job offer in their response to the Our University Graduating Student Questionnaire.

2c. Eighty percent of the accounting program graduates responding to the Our University Recent Alumni survey will indicate that they are employed in a "directly career related" position.

3a. Baccalaureate accounting program graduates will be required to complete successfully (as judged by a jury of faculty from the department) a major accounting project utilizing microcomputer applications during one of several classes in their last semester at the university.

3b. Seventy-five percent of accounting graduates will "agree" or "strongly agree" with the statement "I feel very comfortable in an automated accounting environment" on the Our University Graduating Student Questionnaire.

Figure 11

Your Community College
Transfer Program

**Example of Linkage between
Expanded Statement of Institutional Purpose,
Departmental/Program Intended Outcomes/Objectives,
and Assessment Criteria and Procedures**

**Expanded Statement of
Institutional Purpose**

Mission Statement:

Your Community College is an open-admission, community-based, comprehensive college designed to provide inexpensive, quality educational opportunities (college transfer, career/technical and continuing education) to residents of a five-county service area in the central portion of the Magnolia State.

Goal Statements:

Serve traditional students seeking the first two years of instruction leading to a bachelor's degree.

a. Recipients of the Associate of Arts (AA) or the Associate of Science (AS) degree will be readily accepted at all public universities in the Magnolia State.

b. Graduates with the AA/AS degree will complete their bachelor's degrees at almost the same rate and in about as much time as students completing their entire degree at four-year institutions in the state.

c. Courses offered at the College as a foundation or prerequisite for courses at four-year colleges will be fully accepted for that purpose.

**Departmental/Program
Intended
Outcomes/Objectives**

1. Students transferring will find courses taken at Your Community College fully accepted as the prerequisites for junior and senior level courses at four-year colleges.

2. After one year of adjustment to the four-year college, the grades of students transferring from Your Community College will be similar to those of students who initially enrolled at four-year colleges.

3. Students completing the two-year course of study leading toward transfer to a four-year college as a full-time student will complete their baccalaureate degree at almost the same rate as those students originally enrolling at the four-year college.

**Assessment Criteria
& Procedures**

1a. Ninety percent of those students responding to a follow-up survey one year after transfer to a four-year institution will respond that all their Your Community College courses were accepted as prerequisites for junior and senior level courses.

1b. Each year one of the college's six academic departments will contact their counterparts at the three four-year institutions to whom most College students transfer and all of the courses designed by the department to support the transfer of students will be found to be fully accepted as prerequisites by the four-year institution contacted.

2a. Analysis of data received by Your Community College concerning the grades of students transferring to its primary three four-year colleges will indicate that the difference each semester between the average of such transfer students' GPA's and that of students originally enrolling at the four-year college is statistically insignificant one year after the transfer students' enrollment at the four-year college.

3a. Analysis of data received from each of Your Community Colleges' three primary transfer student destinations will indicate that the difference in the average number of semesters to baccalaureate degree completion of full-time transfer students from Your Community College and students originally enrolling at each four-year college is statistically insignificant.

Figure 12

Your Community College
Automotive Technology Program

Example of Linkage between
Expanded Statement of Institutional Purpose,
Departmental/Program Intended Outcomes/Objectives,
and Assessment Criteria and Procedures

Expanded Statement of Institutional Purpose	Departmental/Program Intended Outcomes/Objectives	Assessment Criteria & Procedures
Mission Statement: Your Community College is an open-admission, community-based, comprehensive college designed to provide inexpensive, quality educational opportunities (college transfer, career/technical and continuing education) to residents of a five-county service area in the central portion of the Magnolia State.	1. Graduates of the Automotive Technology Program will be successfully employed in the field.	1a. Fifty percent of the graduates of the Automotive Technology Program will report employment in the field on the Graduating Student Survey administered at the time of program completion.
		1b. Eighty percent of the graduates of the Automotive Technology Program will report employment in the field on the Recent Alumni Survey distributed one year after graduation.
Goal Statements: Serve persons of all ages in preparing for job entry and careers in a variety of fields.	2. Graduates of the Automotive Technology Program will be technically proficient.	2a. At the close of their final term, 90% of the graduates will be able to identify and correct within a given period of time all of the mechanical problems in five test cars that have been "prepared" for the students by Automotive Technology Program faculty.
a. Recipients of an Associate of Applied Science (AAS) degree will be well prepared for first or entry-level positions in a career field.	3. Employers of the Automotive Technology Program graduates in the five-county service area will be pleased with the education received by their employees	3a. Eighty percent of the automotive respondents to an Employer Survey conducted every 3 years by the college will respond that they would be pleased to employ future graduates of the Automotive Technology Program.
b. College AAS degree programs will be focused on career-related opportunities for graduates in the five-county area.		3b. Fifty percent of automotive employers registered with the College Placement Service will make at least one offer to a graduate of the Automotive Technology program each year.
c. The majority of AAS graduates will find employment in the five-county area.		

- In all four examples, the criteria for program success (average, percentage, etc.) have been identified in conjunction with the means of assessment. It is possible that the criteria might have been identified in the statement of Intended Educational Outcomes.
- One of these three column examples can constitute a department's assessment plan which is the current general expectation of regional accreditation associations with the exception of the Southern Association of Colleges and Schools that requires more of its institutions based upon the longer history of implementation in that region.

Concluding Comments Regarding Assessment

In summary, several points concerning assessment should be borne in mind:

- Assessment activities should be perceived as a means toward improvement of academic programming not an end in themselves.
- Assessment results find their primary meaning in relationship to intended educational (student) outcomes.
- Assessment activities, while detailed and occasionally technical, are not beyond the grasp or comprehension of faculty when accomplished with a desirable level of simplicity.
- While faculty have a vital interest in assessment, providing the coordination and logistical support to see that assessment gets done is an administrative responsibility.

When unmasked and openly discussed, assessment is far from the threat frequently asserted. By working together and establishing a clear understanding concerning intentions, limitations, and roles, departmental faculty and administrators can establish a workable assessment program serving the interest of all concerned.

References

El-Khawas, E. (July, 1993). *Campus Trends*. Higher Education Panel No. 83. Washington, DC: American Council on Education.

Ewell, P. T. (1987). Establishing a campus-based assessment program. In D. F. Halpern (ed.), *Student Outcomes Assessment: What Institutions Stand to Gain* (pp. 9-24). San Francisco: Jossey-Bass.

Chapter IV

CLOSING THE LOOP TO SHOW USE OF ASSESSMENT RESULTS TO IMPROVE INSTRUCTIONAL PROGRAMMING

The end product of virtually all assessment activities (except some accountability initiatives) is the improvement of academic programming based upon the use of assessment results. Without being able to demonstrate such use of assessment results, all previous activities fall short of their intended purpose.

The communication of assessment results to the departmental level is the first step toward its use. The case study institutions indicated that among the least effective means of communication of assessment results to the departmental level was the forwarding of voluminous amounts of tabular data. Verbal communication of results was reported somewhat more effective than tabular presentations. However, the most effective means of communicating assessment results to faculty in academic departments was found to be in summary form with graphic support of tabular data presented orally at departmental faculty meetings (see Chapter III, *Assessment Case Studies*).

Receipt of assessment results usually initiates one of three actions by the department. First, improvement in the means of assessment or restructuring of the statement of intended educational outcomes. Second, the decision to take no curricular action based upon assessment findings indicating accomplishment of intended educational (student) outcomes. Third, utilization of the assessment data to change and improve the performance of its programs and its students.

When changes in programming were made at the case study institutions, they tended to be of two types: "what we teach" and "how we teach." Those changes related to "what we teach" included closer alignment of course offerings with the requirements of the "world of work," or restructuring of the sequence of the curriculum to lead more logically from one subject to another where appropriate. The changes reported in "How we teach" were as numerous as the departments and institutions responding to our inquiries in the preparation of *Assessment Case Studies*. In general, it was reported that different instructional techniques were being used to facilitate student learning and that the majority of these techniques (use of audiovisual aids, interactive computing, increased laboratory experiences, and increased homework) required the student to become a more active participant in the learning process.

Documentation of the use of assessment results should be planned early in the assessment process. Responsibility for maintaining this documentation is probably best lodged at the departmental level with copies forwarded for information only purposes to a central clearinghouse at the institutional level. Normally, the departmental administrator charged with implementation will also have responsibility for documentation for the use of results.

The key concepts in documentation of the use of results are to clearly relate the use back to the intended educational outcomes and to keep the documentation at a minimum of effort. The format suggested in the Assessment Record Book shown in Appendices A and B should suffice for most purposes for each academic program in the department.

Figures 13-16 depict the full "five-column model" tracing development from the Expanded Statement of Institutional Purpose, through programmatic statements of Intended Educational Outcomes, as measured by specified Means of Assessment in relationship to preestablished criteria for program success and ultimately into actual Use of Results to improve programming.

The format shown in Appendix A, the Assessment Record Book, is a narrative adaptation of the graphic portrayal of this linkage shown in Figures 13-16. Each of the components in these figures is included on the Assessment Record Sheet shown in Appendix A. In order to document completely its assessment activities, each department should complete one set of assessment records annually for each academic program of the department. Forms A, B, and C provided in Appendix A, as well as the instructions for their completion are intended to be removed from this publication, photocopied, and used on campuses. Permission for such photocopying and use is herewith granted by the author, who holds the copyright on this publication. Appendix B is provided to illustrate an example of adaptation of one of the graphic representations or "five-column models," as in Figure 13, to the more narrative format contained in the Assessment Record Book.

By whatever means is chosen, a clear expectation in the mind of the public and its representatives is that institutions will be able to document not only their plans for assessment, but the actual results and how these results were used to improve programming.

Figure 13

Undergraduate English Program

Example of Linkage between Expanded Statement of Institutional Purpose, Departmental/Program Intended Outcomes/Objectives, Results, and Use of Results at Our University

Expanded Statement of Institutional Purpose	Departmental/Program Intended Outcomes/Objectives	Assessment Criteria & Procedures	Assessment Results	Use of Results
Mission Statement: The principal focus of Our University's curricular program is undergraduate education in the liberal arts and sciences combined with a number of directly career related and preprofessional fields.	1. Students completing the baccalaureate program in English will compare very favorably in their knowledge of literature with those students completing a similar program nationally.	1a. The average score of the graduates of the baccalaureate program in English on the "Literature in English" MFAT subject test (which they will be required to take shortly before graduation) will be at or near the 50th percentile compared to national results.	1a. MFAT score for this year's graduates (18) found to be at 37th percentile primarily due to the 23rd percentile score on "American Literature" scale.	1a. Course offerings in "American Literature" are being reviewed for consistency with MFAT technical description and items.
		1b. Ninety percent of the English baccalaureate program will "agree" or "strongly agree" with the statement "In the field of literature I feel as well prepared as the majority of individuals nationwide who have completed a similar degree during the past year."	1b. Ninety-three percent responded "agree" or "strongly agree."	1b. No change required.
Goal Statements: Each graduate of Our University will be treated as an individual, and all graduates of baccalaureate-level programs at the University will have developed a depth of understanding in their major field and been afforded the opportunity to prepare for a career or profession following graduation.	2. Graduates will be able to critique a brief draft essay, pointing out the grammatical, spelling, and punctuation errors, and offering appropriate suggestions for correction of the deficiencies.	2a. As part of a departmental comprehensive examination administered during the students' final semester prior to graduation, they will critique a short draft essay, identify grammatical, spelling, and punctuation errors; and offer suggestions for correction of the deficiencies. Eighty percent of the program's graduates will identify and offer suggestions for remediation of 90% of the errors in the draft essay.	2a. Ninety-two percent of graduates identified 87% of errors. However, grammatical conventions regarding capitalization were not consistently applied.	2a. Faculty use of commonly accepted conventions regarding capitalization in reviewing upper division papers is being emphasized.
				2b. No action required.
	3. Students completing the baccalaureate program will be capable of writing a brief journal article and having it published.	3a. All graduates of the baccalaureate level program in English will prepare a journal article for submission and forward it to the English department.	3a. Article received from all (18) graduates.	3a. No action required.
		3b. Eighty percent of those journal articles submitted will be judged acceptable for publication by a jury of English department faculty from an institution comparable to Our University.	3b. Fifty-five percent of articles reviewed were found acceptable for publication.	3b. English 407 (advanced writing) is being modified to include journal article exercises.
		3c. Twenty percent of those articles submitted will be published in student or other publications.	3c. Thirty percent of articles were published.	3c. No action required.

Figure 14

Accounting Degree Program

Example of Linkage between Expanded Statement of Institutional Purpose, Departmental/Program Intended Outcomes/Objectives, Assessment Criteria and Procedures, Results, and Use of Results at Our University

Expanded Statement of Institutional Purpose	Departmental/Program Intended Outcomes/Objectives	Assessment Criteria & Procedures	Assessment Results	Use of Results
Mission Statement: The principal focus of Our University's curricular program is undergraduate education in the liberal arts and sciences, combined with a number of directly career related and preprofessional fields.	1. Students completing the baccalaureate program in accounting will be well prepared for their first position in the field.	1a. Eighty percent of those taking the CPA exam each year and indicating an accounting degree from Our University will pass three of four parts on the exam.	1a. Seventy percent of those taking the CPA exam passed all four parts. Ninety percent passed three of four parts. Seventy-five percent passed the auditing portion.	1a. Method of teaching auditing being revised by faculty.
		1b. Eighty-five percent of the graduates of the accounting baccalaureate program will "agree" or "strongly agree" with the statement "I am well prepared for my first position" contained in Our University's Graduating Student Questionnaire.	1b. Ninety responded "agree" or "strongly agree."	1b. No action required.
		1c. Employers of accounting program graduates hired through the Our University Placement Service will indicate on a survey forwarded to them by the Placement Service one year after employment of the graduate, an average rating of 7.5 or more (on a scale of 1-10) in response to the question "How well was your employee prepared for their position by Our University?"	1c. Average ranking of 8.3 was recorded, but bimodal frequency distribution encountered.	1c. Follow-up telephone interview being conducted with all employers rating 6.0 or lower.
Goal Statements: All graduates of baccalaureate programs will have developed a depth of understanding in their major field and been afforded the opportunity to prepare for a career following graduation.	2. Baccalaureate graduates of the accounting program will find ready employment in the field.	2a. Ninety percent of accounting graduates registered with the placement service each fall will have received a job offer by the close of spring semester each year.	2a. Ninety-five percent received a job offer or currently employed.	2a. No action required.
		2b. Sixty percent of students completing the accounting degree program will indicate that they are currently employed or have accepted a job offer in their response to the Our University Graduating Student Questionnaire.	2b. Eighty percent indicated receipt of job offer.	2b. Criterion being raised to 80%.
		2c. Eighty percent of the accounting program graduates responding to the Our University Recent Alumni survey will indicate that they are employed in a "directly career related" position.	2c. Ninety percent indicated employment.	2c. No action required.
	3. Graduates will be experienced in the use of microcomputers for accounting procedures.	3a. Baccalaureate accounting program graduates will be required to complete successfully (as judged by a jury of faculty from the department) a major accounting project utilizing microcomputer applications during one of several classes in their last semester at the university.	3a. Sixty percent of graduates' projects were judged acceptable on first review by faculty panel.	3a. More microcomputer applications are being integrated into core of Accounting classes.
		3b. Seventy-five percent of accounting graduates will "agree" or "strongly agree" with the statement "I feel very comfortable in an automated accounting environment" on the Our University Graduating Student Questionnaire.	3b. Eighty percent indicated "agree" or "strongly agree."	3b. No action required.

Figure 15

Your Community College Transfer Program

Example of Linkage between
Expanded Statement of Institutional Purpose,
Departmental/Program Intended Outcomes/Objectives,
Assessment Criteria and Procedures, Results, and Use of Results

Expanded Statement of Institutional Purpose	Departmental/Program Intended Outcomes/Objectives	Assessment Criteria & Procedures	Assessment Results	Use of Results
Mission Statement: Your Community College is an open-admission, community-based, comprehensive college designed to provide inexpensive, quality educational opportunities (college transfer, career/technical and continuing education) to residents of a five-county service area in the central portion of the Magnolia State.	1. Students transferring will find courses taken at Your Community College fully accepted as the prerequisites for junior and senior level courses at four-year colleges.	1a. Ninety percent of those students responding to a follow-up survey one year after transfer to a four-year institution will respond that all their Your Community College courses were accepted as prerequisites for junior and senior level courses.	1a. Ninety-five percent of responding students reported acceptance.	1a. No action necessary.
Goal Statements: Serve traditional students seeking the first two years of instruction leading to a bachelor's degree.		1b. Each year one of the college's six academic departments will contact their counterparts at the three four-year institutions to whom most College students transfer and all of the courses designed by the department to support the transfer of students will be found to be fully accepted as prerequisites by the four-year institution contacted.	1b. Problem noted in change of introductory accounting course to microcomputer assisted at two of three primary transfer institutions.	1b. Expansion of microcomputer utilization in introductory accounting problems at Your Community College is underway.
a. Recipients of the Associate of Arts (AA) or the Associate of Science (AS) degree will be readily accepted at all public universities in the Magnolia State.	2. After one year of adjustment to the four-year college, the grades of students transferring from Your Community College will be similar to those of students who initially enrolled at four-year colleges.	2a. Analysis of data received by Your Community College concerning the grades of students transferring to its primary three four-year colleges will indicate that the difference each semester between the average of such transfer students' GPA's and that of students originally enrolling at the four-year college is statistically insignificant one year after the transfer students' enrollment at the four-year college.	2a. Overall GPA of Your Community College transfers found to be slightly (not significant) less than native students, but significantly less in math classes.	2a. Math 107 (college algebra) is being strengthened to better relate with calculus at Four-year institutions.
b. Graduates with the AA/AS degree will complete their bachelor's degrees at almost the same rate and in about as much time as students completing their entire degree at four-year institutions in the state.	3. Students completing the two-year course of study leading toward transfer to a four-year college as a full-time student will complete their baccalaureate degree at almost the same rate as those students originally enrolling at the four-year college.	3a. Analysis of data received from each of Your Community Colleges' three primary transfer student destinations will indicate that the difference in the average number of semesters to baccalaureate degree completion of full-time transfer students from Your Community College and students originally enrolling at each four-year college is statistically insignificant.	3a. Degree completion time of Your Community College transfer students found to be virtually identical to native students.	3a. No change necessary.
c. Courses offered at the College as a foundation or prerequisite for courses at four-year colleges will be fully accepted for that purpose.				

Figure 16

Your Community College
Automotive Technology Program

Example of Linkage between
Expanded Statement of Institutional Purpose,
Departmental/Program Intended Outcomes/Objectives,
Assessment Criteria and Procedures, Results, and Use of Results

Expanded Statement of Institutional Purpose	Departmental/Program Intended Outcomes/Objectives	Assessment Criteria & Procedures	Assessment Results	Use of Results
Mission Statement: Your Community College is an open-admission, community-based, comprehensive college designed to provide inexpensive, quality educational opportunities (college transfer, career/technical and continuing education) to residents of a five-county service area in the central portion of the Magnolia State. **Goal Statements:** Serve persons of all ages in preparing for job entry and careers in a variety of fields. a. Recipients of an Associate of Applied Science (AAS) degree will be well prepared for first or entry-level positions in a career field. b. College AAS degree programs will be focused on career-related opportunities for graduates in the five-county area. c. The majority of AAS graduates will find employment in the five-county area.	1. Graduates of the Automotive Technology Program will be successfully employed in the field. 2. Graduates of the Automotive Technology Program will be technically proficient. 3. Employers of the Automotive Technology Program graduates in the five-county service area will be pleased with the education received by their employees.	1a. Fifty percent of the graduates of the Automotive Technology Program will report employment in the field on the Graduating Student Survey administered at the time of program completion. 1b. Eighty percent of the graduates of the Automotive Technology Program will report employment in the field on the Recent Alumni Survey distributed one year after graduation. 2a. At the close of their final term, 90% of the graduates will be able to identify and correct within a given period of time all of the mechanical problems in five test cars that have been "prepared" for the students by Automotive Technology Program faculty. 2b. Eighty percent of Automotive Technology Program graduates will pass the National Automotive Test. 3a. Eighty percent of the automotive respondents to an Employer Survey conducted every 3 years by the college will respond that they would be pleased to employ future graduates of the Automotive Technology Program. 3b. Fifty percent of automotive employers registered with the College Placement Service will make at least one offer to a graduate of the Automotive Technology program each year.	1a. Seventy percent reported employment. 1b. Eighty percent reported employment. 2a. Eighty percent success rate. Most failures could not find problem in electrical system. 2b. Eighty-three percent pass rate on National Automotive Test - Weakness in items regarding hydraulic theory. 3a. Ninety percent reported willingness to employ, but only 50% of body shops. 3b. Eighty percent of employers registered had made a job offer.	1a. No action necessary. 1b. No action necessary. 2a. Expanded Electrical Trouble Shooting Component of AT 202 Automotive Electrical Systems. 2b. Modified means of teaching hydraulic theory in AT 102 Basic Auto Systems. 3a. Added body shop representative to Advisory Committee and are reviewing curriculum to determine if separate program is needed. 3b. No action necessary.

IMPLEMENTATION OF INSTITUTIONAL EFFECTIVENESS WITHIN ADMINISTRATIVE OR EDUCATIONAL SUPPORT DEPARTMENTS

Karen W. Nichols

Why Is an Administrative or Educational Support Department Involved in the Assessment Movement?

Only within the context of comprehensive implementation of institutional effectiveness operations will most nonacademic departments become involved in assessment. This circumstance is most likely to occur with institutional preparation for reaffirmation of regional accreditation. Within that process, the academic sector of the institution will undoubtedly be the center ring in the circus; however, administrative and educational support departments will also be expected to take part in the process of supporting the Expanded Statement of Institutional Purpose.

Administrative and educational support departments will be expected to provide evidence that their operations support, directly or indirectly, implementation of the Expanded Statement of Institutional Purpose by attaining departmental intended administrative objectives. To do so, departments will need to: (a) formulate objectives similar in some ways to those statements of intended educational (student) outcomes prepared by academic programs; (b) indicate how those objectives support or link to the institution's Expanded Statement of Institutional Purpose or the administrative unit's mission or statement of purpose; (c) demonstrate that their unit administrative objectives are being accomplished; and/or (d) use the results of assessment to improve administrative or educational support operations. While this requirement is similar to that placed upon academic programs, there are important differences identified in the succeeding paragraphs.

Relationship to Expanded Statement of Institutional Purpose
One substantial difference that may exist between intended educational outcomes and administrative objectives is the manner in which they support the statement of purpose for the institution. While it is recommended that statements

of intended educational outcomes relate directly to the Expanded Statement Institutional of Purpose and avoid separate mission statements at the department, college, division, etc., levels to simplify the process, it may be necessary for statements of administrative objectives to be linked with an administrative unit mission statement which in turn supports the overall Expanded Statement of Institutional Purpose. This is likely to transpire when the statement of purpose for the institution is less than specific about the role of administrative and educational support units in accomplishing its mission or when required by a regional accrediting association, such as the change made in December 1994 by the Southern Association of Colleges and Schools. When possible, it is recommended that, as in the case of intended educational outcomes, administrative objectives be tied directly to and support the Expanded Statement of Institutional Purpose. However, when this is not possible an arrangement as shown below and in Figure 17 (page 63) is appropriate.

(Extract from Student Affairs Division Mission Statement)
Expanded Statement of Institutional Purpose

To provide services which assist students in selecting their vocation and making the transition into the world of work.

Preparing Statements of Administrative Objectives

Each administrative or educational support department (separately organized unit) will need to establish its own set of administrative objectives. These statements will, by the nature of the work done in these units, be more "process" than student "outcomes" oriented (see discussion "Results vs. Process," page 18). There frankly is little that can be stated in terms of educational (student) outcomes about the vital functions of the office of the registrar or physical plant. Hence, the administrative objectives established will primarily describe what the department is going to do and only to a lesser extent what its impact (results) will be on clientele (students, etc.). However, whenever feasible, administrative and educational support units should establish results-oriented statements regarding their own operations.

Is This Management by Objectives (MBO)?

Yes and no. Yes, this is related to certain aspects of MBO as practiced in some institutions of higher learning in that departments are asked to identify their objectives and then determine if those objectives are being met. No, in several other important regards.

First, there is no intention that individuals within nonacademic units establish separate objectives for each person or function. Rather, the professional staff in each unit should work together with the department head to establish a limited number of overarching objectives for the unit as a whole (see discussion regarding "How many" on pages 25–26).

Second, the objectives established are separate from the institution's personnel evaluation process and resource (funding) request/allocation cycle. Within institutional effectiveness, departments (academic and nonacademic) are free to stretch themselves to the limit and to attempt innovative approaches to providing services without fear of failure. Within institutional effectiveness, departments are not held accountable for failure or success, only for having in place a process for stating objectives, measuring accomplishments, and using the results to improve programming. Further, since this process is separate from resource acquisition or allocation, departments need not focus primarily on objectives that will result in increased funding, but upon basic operations of underlying importance to departmental and institutional effectiveness.

Third, when possible, statements of administrative objectives should focus upon the results of administrative or educational support operations rather than the processes themselves. MBO applications in higher education have focused exclusively on "what we will do." While much of the effort to implement institutional effectiveness support will, by the nature of the services provided by the unit, focus upon process, the impact of these efforts should be stated in results-oriented terms whenever possible. Hence, rather than the office of the registrar setting an objective related to improved handling of transcript request, an administrative objective stating that, e.g., "95% of transcript requests will be processed and mailed within 72 hours of their receipt" should be formulated. Rather than the physical plant setting as an objective—"Three buildings will be brought into the institution's Energy Management System (EMS)"—the administrative objective set might state: "As a result of three buildings being brought within the institutions EMS, $18,000 annually will be avoided in utility expenditures for these buildings."

How Does This Effort Relate to Total Quality Management (TQM) or Continuous Quality Improvement (CQI)?

The procedures outlined herein regarding assessment activities in nonacademic or educational support units are in concert with the tenets of TQM or CQI as described by most authorities (See resource section "Assessment of Continuous Quality Improvement" by Elfner in *A Practitioner's Handbook* [3rd ed.]). The primary differences between these mutually supportive processes of outcomes assessment and TQM/CQI relate to the focus in the instructional area of assessment on outcomes (end of production) and that of TQM/CQI on the processes engaged in production (i.e., teaching). Because a great majority of educational support and administrative objectives are already process-oriented due to the nature of their functions, this difference is moot, under these circumstances, and assessment and TQM/CQI are even more closely related.

If an administrative or educational support unit is in the process of implementing a program of Total Quality Management or Continuous Quality

Improvement, that program should be allowed to continue without interruption, as its result will be very similar to that proposed in this publication, although there may need to be some minor changes in description of procedures in order to meet regional accreditation requirements.

What Do Such Statements of Administrative Objectives Look Like?

Figure 17, on the following page, provides an example of three statements of administrative objectives for the Career Services Center in the second column from the left. Note that the first of these administrative objectives retains a large measure of outcomes or results orientation, while the last two are clearly process-related.

Means of Assessment in Administrative and Educational Support Departments
Once a department has identified its administrative objectives it should next (or simultaneously) consider means for assessment of their accomplishment. Because assessment remains more of an art than a science, it is important that departments identify several means of assessment for each administrative objective to counter what may be inconsistencies in any single means of assessment.

The means of assessment most frequently identified with nonacademic departments include clientele satisfaction or attitude, direct measures or counts of departmental operations, and the use of an external evaluator.

Attitudinal Measures of Client Satisfaction
Since most administrative or educational support departments do not operate on a profit basis or contribute in a clearly discernible way to student learning, satisfaction of clientele with services provided is one of the primary means of assessment available. These attitudes can be gauged either one at a time (a detailed questionnaire regarding services administered to clients at the "point of contact" or provision of services) or as general levels of satisfaction with specific services (library, bookstore, etc.) in a composite institutional survey of enrolled students or graduates.

Unless there is substantial reason to believe that an individual departmental data gathering effort is required (detailed questionnaire, structure interview, etc.) general levels of client satisfaction should suffice for most assessment purposes in nonacademic departments. If a number of individual clientele satisfaction measures are initiated on the campus, they will need to be carefully coordinated to avoid asking students to respond to the same inquiries more than once. In general, nonacademic departments should avoid construction, annual dissemination, and analysis of attitudinal questionnaires themselves. They should seek assistance from and support of the institutional research component on the campus.

Regardless of which approach is utilized to gather clientele satisfaction information, the point of contact or composite, the validity of clientele responses will

Figure 17

Career Services Center

Example of Linkage between Expanded Statement of Institutional Purpose, Departmental/Program Intended Outcomes/Objectives, Assessment Criteria and Procedures, Results, and Use of Results at Our University

Expanded Statement of Institutional Purpose	Departmental/Program Intended Outcomes/Objectives	Assessment Criteria & Procedures	Assessment Results	Use of Results
Our University Mission Statement: We also seek to provide a supportive and challenging environment in which students can realize the full potential of their abilities.	1. Of those graduates seeking employment, at least half will have been offered a job prior to leaving the University.	1a. A follow-up survey of Career Services Center registrants will indicate that of those students responding, 40% had received a job offer by October after graduation.	1a. 43% of those responding indicated receipt of a job offer.	1a. No action required.
		1b. Of those students seeking to be employed after graduation, on the Graduating Student Survey, 50% will indicate that they were already employed or had received a job offer.	1b. 32% indicated employment or receipt of a job offer.	1b. Efforts to encourage student registration with Career Services Center increased. A computer job listing program was placed on-line for student access.
	2. Offer an increasing number of job search strategy workshops each year that are attended by more students annually.	2a. Records maintained will indicate more job search workshops offered each academic year.	2a. Records indicate the offering of three more job strategy workshops this past academic year than during the previous academic year.	2a. No action required.
		2b. Records maintained will indicate an increase in the number of students attending job strategy workshops each year.	2b. Attendance at job search strategy workshops declined by 7% this past academic year.	2b. Increase articles concerning career issues in student newspaper. Development of a career information peer group to provide information to fraternities and sororities.
Extract from Student Affairs Division Mission Statement: To provide services which assist students in selecting their vocation and making the transition into the world of work.	3. Clients will be pleased with the services received from the Career Services Center.	3a. The level of satisfaction with the Career Services Center expressed by students on the Graduating Student Survey will exceed that for overall student services.	3a. This past academic year, graduating students rated overall student services 3.2 on a satisfaction scale from 1-5 and the Career Center 3.4.	3a. No action required.
		3b. 96% of students completing a point of contact survey at the close of the job search strategy workshop will "agree" or "strongly agree" with the statement "This workshop fulfilled my expectations and provided clear, useful advice in the job search."	3b. 83% of past academic year respondents "agreed" or "strongly agreed." Workshops presented by one employee rated only 63% on average.	3b. Solicited feedback regarding presentation improvement from career information peer group. One presenter rehearsed and videotaped to improve presentation.

remain a question. Few institutions will find students rate highly their food service, registrar, bursar, or parking on their campuses. The primary issue in attitudes regarding the services provided by these departments is one of relativity. Do our student's dislike the food service at this institution more than do students at other institutions?

This desirability of comparing campus clientele satisfaction indications such as those described above with those of other institutions appears to support the utilization of standardized attitudinal surveys which provide normative response patterns (see Resource Section by Raines, Bridger, and Wolff in *A Practitioner's Handbook* [3rd ed.]). However, by carefully reviewing standardized items and normative response patterns, even locally developed instruments can provide some indirect insight into reactions regarding similar subjects at other institutions.

Direct Measures or Counts of Departmental Operations
In many cases, statements of administrative objectives will relate to a volume of activity (number of students registered), level of efficiency (average time for student completion of the open registration process), or a measure of performance quality (average errors noted per transcript audit). In such instances, administrative or education support units should seek to identify performance standards having some basis in their professional areas (counselors per hundred students, processing time for purchase orders, etc.) where available, and establish mechanisms for the collection of the information necessary for assessment. (See resource section "Setting and Evaluating Objectives and Outcomes in Nonacademic Units" by Donald Reichard in *A Practitioner's Handbook* [3rd ed.].)

Use of the External Evaluator
While it is not feasible every year, it is a good policy to occasionally engage a nationally or regionally recognized external evaluator or consultant to review nonacademic or educational support operations. Such an evaluation is particularly useful to the institution in objectively reconciling institutional expectations, resources available, constituent satisfaction, and departmental operations with commonly identified good or acceptable practices in the field. Care should be taken to select a genuinely neutral external evaluator to protect the institution's and department's interests. The reports of other external evaluators such as auditors, OSHA inspectors, fire marshals, and health department inspectors may also be utilized as means of assessment.

Example of Institutional Effectiveness Implementation in Administrative or Educational Support Departments
Figure 17 illustrates the full five-column model through Use of Assessment Results for the Career Services Center at the hypothetical institution, Our University. Note that in addition to identifying the Career Services Center administrative objectives and means of assessment established by the Career Center

staff, this model depicts hypothetical results and how they were utilized to improve programming, Several aspects of this example bear further comment. First, the example contains criteria for departmental success within the means of assessment identified. It is important that departments include such criteria as a benchmark against which to measure their assessment results. Second, in each case, multiple means of assessment for each administrative objective are identified to provide a more reliable measure of departmental accomplishment. Third, note that when departmental expectations are achieved, no action is required to further improve programming.

In addition to this example, a number of other examples of the second and third columns of this five-column model (administrative objectives and means of assessment and criteria for success) are included at the close of Appendix B in *Assessment Case Studies*.

How Do I Get Started in Implementation in an Educational Support or Administrative Department?

Seek out or locate the most current departmental statement of mission or purpose that lists the various functions your unit performs. Gather at least the professional staff and also in many units the nonprofessional staff and ask the question: "To what extent does this existing unit statement of purpose or mission describe our department's functions at the institution?" Then go about the process of revising or refining the unit mission into operational functions accomplished by the unit. Once these overall functions are agreed upon by the staff, identify what seem to be the most important three to five of these functions from the standpoint of the institution. You might phrase the question as, "If the institution could only have us do three to five of these functions, which would they select?" Following identification of these three to five functions, ask the group, "How can we ascertain how well we are accomplishing these functions?" and "Given current resources, how can we tell if more can be done in this area?" These two questions should begin to elicit the necessary means of assessment and criteria and lead toward establishment of the departmental assessment plan.

Final Comments Regarding Implementation in Administrative and Educational Support Departments

Once administrative and educational support departments realize that their support of the Expanded Statement of Institutional Purpose is necessary, implementation of institutional effectiveness activities in those departments is relatively straightforward. In most instances, the greatest effort will need to be directed toward clarification of general understandings regarding departmental objectives. In many cases, assessment criteria and means will be found to be readily available in a short period of time.

Chapter VI

IF INSTITUTIONAL EFFECTIVENESS OR EDUCATIONAL OUTCOMES ASSESSMENT IS TO WORK, IT MUST DO SO AT THE DEPARTMENTAL LEVEL

Critical Issues in Departmental Implementation

In consulting with more than 100 colleges and universities across the country on this subject and in most instances working at the departmental level within these institutions, a number of critical issues in departmental implementation have been observed by the author. Most of these issues have been addressed earlier in this publication, however, they are commented upon again briefly as a means of summarizing.

Understanding clearly what is expected and what support is available—It is of paramount importance that the departmental implementation "get off to a good start," and in order to do that, a very clear understanding of (a) what is expected of the department and (b) what support is to be provided to the department by the institution is essential.

Faculty involvement: getting it and maintaining it—There are no magic solutions to this issue. Most faculty will become involved in the effort as they are committed to the improvement of student learning in their discipline. However, there are a number of faculty (roughly 25%) whose position on the subject of assessment activities can be described as ranging from passive resistance to outright opposition. The faculty in this latter 25% should publicly be offered the opportunity to take part in the endeavor and then, unless they join in, be ignored as the balance of the department goes about its business of implementation. It has been the author's experience that most members of this recalcitrant group will eventually become involved with the process if they can see that implementation is actually contributing toward the improvement of the curriculum and students' performance.

Focus on Intended Student Outcomes versus Process—The departmental administrator in instructional departments will need to guard carefully against slipping into "process-type" statements of Intended Educational Outcomes, which describe what the instructional department intends to do rather than what the student will be able to think, know, or do. If the statements of Intended Educational (Student) Outcomes for each academic program begin: "The graduate will…," then the tendency toward process type statements will be diminished. Of course in educational support and administrative departments such process-type statements will be commonly found and are entirely appropriate.

***Limiting the number of Statements of Intended Educational Outcomes
being assessed at any one time***—This need has been explained at some length
earlier; however, failure to address this issue and reduce the number of statements of Intended Educational Outcomes upon which assessment will be
focused at one time to between three and five, is absolutely the quickest way to
ensure failure of the process.

***The choice of standardized or locally developed cognitive means of assess-
ment***—In some departments, the choice of these two means of cognitive assessment causes considerable controversy among the faculty. Under these
circumstances, assuming the number of graduates is large enough, have half take
the locally developed measure and the other half the standardized cognitive
means of assessment. If the number of graduates is relatively small, administer
standardized and locally developed instruments in alternating years.

Utilization of a breadth of means of assessment—Unfortunately, many times
the means of assessment identified extend only as far as cognitive means of assessment. While there is no requirement, departmental administrators will want to
attempt to also utilize attitudinal, behavioral, and performance measures as there are
a number of intended educational outcomes not related to cognitive assessment.

Gaining student commitment to assessment activities—Case study institutions
reported embedding means of assessment within Capstone or other courses as the
best means for gaining student commitment to take assessment activities seriously.
See *Assessment Case Studies* for other suggestions regarding this important issue.

Keeping departmental cost to a minimum—There is no better means of
keeping the primary departmental costs—the investment of faculty members'
time—to a minimum than limiting the number of Statements of Intended Educational Outcomes upon which assessment is going to be focused at any one time.
Some additional out-of-pocket costs at the departmental level can be expected;
however, it is recommended that these out-of-pocket costs for assessment activities be funded from a central account under the control of whoever is responsible
for assessment implementation on the campus.

***Use and documentation of use of assessment results to improve academic
programming***—Nothing will stop assessment activities quite as quickly as the
apparent misuse of assessment data to make decisions concerning individuals.
Above all, institutional effectiveness assessment must be separated from evaluation activities related to promotion of individuals or retention of academic programs. Documentation of the use of assessment results is suggested based upon
utilization of the "Assessment Record Book" provided in Appendix A.

***Maintaining the process over time through transitions in departmental
leadership***—This long-term problem will need to be acknowledged at the institutional level, and periodically a reeducation and updating of departmental
assessment leaders will need to take place.

Concluding Comments

Like so many other matters within our institutions, successful implementation of institutional effectiveness or educational (student) outcomes assessment is only possible when it is based upon the efforts of faculty and staff at the departmental level. The departmental administrator who must already prepare the next semester's class schedule; forward recommendations for tenure, promotions, etc.; make decisions concerning the department's budget; and attend innumerable meetings now has one more responsibility—implementation of institutional effectiveness or educational outcomes assessment activities within the department. While the central administration of the institution surely should provide the technical and logistical support services for assessment, these services can only facilitate the work that must be done in the institution's departments and programs.

As you've read through this publication, you have undoubtedly begun to appreciate that some degree of effort will be involved in departmental implementation within any of the contexts described. Several themes regarding the nature of the effort which you are about to put forth have been repeated in various ways throughout this publication. These are:

- Make absolutely certain of what is being requested of your department and understand the implications of that request.
- Involve faculty (as well as professional staff) in identification of intended educational (student) outcomes and administrative objectives.
- Assessment activities are distinctly accomplishable without high levels of statistical or research expertise.
- Keep the entire process as simple as possible. Far better to complete a relatively modest plan for implementation than to fail to complete a very sophisticated design requiring backbreaking effort and producing mountains of data.
- Use the results to improve your departmental operations and student learning.

The "bad news" is that by virtue of having been asked to read *The Departmental Guide and Record Book,* you probably have no choice within your institution as to whether or not to implement educational (student) outcomes assessment or institutional effectiveness support operations linked to your institutional statement of purpose by your department. The "good news" is twofold: First, what you are being asked to do (through the "three-column model") is accomplishable with modest effort during the course of a year, considerable effort in six months, and substantial effort in three months. Second, the results of your effort can be utilized to genuinely improve student learning and department operations.

As in many things in life, implementation is not an option, but a requirement. Whether we make of it a burdensome chore or an opportunity to improve the department or program we cherish is up to each departmental administrator.

ASSESSMENT RECORD BOOK FORMS AND INSTRUCTIONS FOR COMPLETION

The following instructions relate to Forms A, B, and C, shown in succession on the following pages. They may be reproduced without special permission and are designed to be enlarged by approximately one-third so as to fit on 8½ x 11 copy paper. When completed, these forms collectively constitute the Assessment Record Book for each department.

Instructions for Form A:

- In the blank at the top of the page, provide the complete name of the instructional (academic) or administrative/educational support department which this set of assessment records describes. There should be one Assessment Record Book (containing one or more sets of assessment records—Forms B & C and one form A) for each department at the institution.
- Indicate the period of time covered by this form. Initially this period may cover a number of years until the first use of results is recorded. After that time, the Assessment Record Books will be completed either annually or as frequently as departments are required to report.
- If this Assessment Record Book is being completed for a noninstructional administrative/ educational support department indicating administrative objectives, circle "yes" in line "a." For instructional (academic) departments, circle "no" and complete the title of each degree program (major) and degree level (bachelor's, master's, specialist, doctorate) of each degree program offered in the academic department below line "b."

Instructions for Form B:

- Instructional (academic) departments should fill in the blank provided at the top of the page, with the title and level of the degree program (major) for which this Form B is intended. One such Form B should be prepared for **each** degree program listed by the instructional department on Form A. Administrative/educational support departments should list only the name of the department as indicated at the top of the Form A previously completed.
- Indicate period of time covered by this form.
- In the portion of the form referencing the Expanded Statement of Institutional Purpose, indicate in the box entitled "Mission" which portion of the institution's overall mission the instructional degree program or administrative/educational support department supports. In the portion of the form referencing the Expanded Statement of Institutional Purpose, provide in the box identified as "Goal(s)" those specific institutional goals included as part of the Expanded Statement of Instructional Purpose that this instructional degree program or administrative/educational support department supports. In the limited number of occasions when an administrative department is required to link its administrative objectives to an administrative department mission statement, an extract from that administrative department mission statement should be included in the section marked "Goal(s)" (see discussion starting on page 59).
- In the portion of the form identified as Intended Educational (Student) Research or Public Service Outcomes, or Departmental Administrative (Educational) Objectives list the intended educational outcomes for academic programs and the administrative objectives for

administrative departments. Each administrative department or instructional program should have no more than three to five intended outcomes or administrative objectives which it is assessing at any one time.

Instructions for Completing Form C:

- Provide the name of the instructional degree program and degree level or administrative department in the blank provided at the top of the page.
- Indicate period of time covered by this form.
- In the area identified as Intended Educational (Student) Research or Public Service Outcome, or Departmental Administrative (Educational) Objective, provide from the bottom of Form B (in the numbered boxes), one intended outcome or objective for this instructional (academic) program or administrative department. There should be as many Form C's as there are listed Intended Educational (Student) Outcomes or Administrative (Educational) Objectives in the numbered boxes on Form B.
- In the area identified as Means of Assessment and Criteria for Success, identify at least one and, where possible, two or more means of assessment to determine the accomplishment of the intended educational (student) outcome or administrative (educational) objective listed in the top box. In addition to describing the means of assessment, the criteria or benchmark for judging the department's or program's success in meeting this intended outcome or objective should be included therein. Note that the means of assessment should be identified by number and letter linking them back to the intended educational (student) outcome or administrative (educational) objective.
- In the portion of the form identified as Assessment Results, describe what took place when the assessment activity identified above (as linked with arrows) actually took place.
- In the portion of the form identified as Use of Results, describe how these results were used to improve academic or administrative programming at the institution. It is distinctly possible that no use may be required based upon the achievement of the intended educational (student) outcomes or administrative (educational) objectives established.

ASSESSMENT RECORD BOOK
FOR DEPARTMENT OF

_____

(Department/Program)

_____

(Period Covered)

Includes Assessment Records for:

a. Administrative/Educational Support Department Only   Yes   No

b. Instructional Degree Programs in this Academic Department Listed Below:

<u>Title of Degree Program</u>	<u>Degree Level</u>
_____	_____
_____	_____
_____	_____
_____	_____
_____	_____
_____	_____
_____	_____
_____	_____
_____	_____

FORM A

ASSESSMENT RECORD
FOR

_____
(Department/Program)

_____
(Period Covered)

Expanded Statement of Institutional Purpose

Mission:

Goal(s):

Intended Educational (Student), Research or Public Service Outcomes, or Departmental Administrative Objectives

1.

2.

3.

4.

5.

Form B

ASSESSMENT RECORD
FOR

(Department/Program)

(Period Covered)

Intended Educational (Student), Research or Public Service Outcome, or Departmental Administrative Objective

NOTE: There should be one form C for each intended objective/outcome listed on form B.

First

a. Means of Assessment & Criteria for Success:

a. Assessment Results:

a. Use of Results:

Second

b. Means of Assessment & Criteria for Success:

b. Assessment Results:

a. Use of Results:

Form C

ASSESSMENT RECORD
FOR

(Department/Program)

(Period Covered)

Intended Educational (Student), Research or Public Service Outcome, or Departmental Administrative Objective

NOTE: There should be one form C for each intended objective/outcome listed on form B.

```
___
```

First
```
___
```
a. Means of Assessment & Criteria for Success:

```
___
```
a. Assessment Results:

```
___
```
a. Use of Results:

Second
```
___
```
b. Means of Assessment & Criteria for Success:

```
___
```
b. Assessment Results:

```
___
```
b. Use of Results:

Third
```
___
```
c. Means of Assessment & Criteria for Success:

```
___
```
c. Assessment Results:

```
___
```
c. Use of Results:

Form C

EXAMPLE ENTRY IN THE ASSESSMENT RECORD BOOK OF UNDERGRADUATE ENGLISH PROGRAM EXAMPLE PROVIDED IN FIGURE 13

Appendix B includes a set of Assessment Record Forms completed for the Undergraduate English Program at Our University, which is Figure 13 (page 55) in this publication. Shown on Form A are all of the instructional degree programs offered by the English Department. On Form B, the specific Undergraduate English Program is related to the Mission and Goals for the institution and the intended educational outcomes are listed in the boxes 1, 2, and 3. Note that there are three completed Form C's in the example provided—one for each educational outcome listed at the bottom of Form B for the Undergraduate English Program. The completed sample Form C's relate each intended educational outcome, means of assessment and criteria for success, actual assessment results, and the use of assessment results in this example. There would be one Form B and three to five Form C's for each instructional (academic) program listed on the English Department's Form A. A general outline for three different departments and degree programs is shown below.

OUTLINE
EXAMPLE OF THE ASSESSMENT RECORD BOOK CONTENTS
(Below are the number and types of forms that comprise the
Assessment Record Book for the different units described)

- Administrative/Educational Support
Department with Four Administrative Objectives
Form A
↓
Form B
↓ ↓ ↓ ↓
Four Form C's

- Instructional Department with One Degree Program
Having Five Intended Educational Outcomes
Form A
↓
Form B
↓ ↓ ↓ ↓ ↓
Five Form C's

- Instructional Department with Three Degree Programs
(With five, four, and three intended educational outcomes, respectively)
Form A
↓
One Form B — One Form B — One Form B
(One for each program)
↙ ↙ ↘ ↘   ↙ ↓ ↘   ↙ ↙ ↓ ↘ ↘
Four Form C's — Three Form C's — Five Form C's

ASSESSMENT RECORD BOOK
FOR

English Department
(Department/Program)

Academic Year 1995-1996
(Period Covered)

Includes Assessment Records for:
a. Administrative/Educational Support Department Only   Yes   No

b. Instructional Degree Programs in this Academic Department Listed Below:

Title of Degree Program	Degree Level
Undergraduate English Program	Bachelor of Arts
English Literature	Master of Arts
English as a Foreign Language	Master of Arts

FORM A

ASSESSMENT RECORD
FOR

Undergraduate English Program
(Department/Program)
Academic Year 1995-1996
(Period Covered)

Expanded Statement of Institutional Purpose

Mission:
The principal focus of Our University's curricular program is undergraduate education in the liberal arts and sciences combined with a number of directly career related and preprofessional fields.

Goal(s): Each graduate of Our University will be treated as an individual, and all graduates of baccalaureate level programs at the University will have developed a depth of understanding in their major field and been afforded the opportunity to prepare for a career or profession following graduation.

Intended Educational (Student), Research or Public Service Outcomes, or Departmental Administrative Objectives

1.
Students completing the baccalaureate program in English will compare very favorably in their knowledge of literature with those students completing a similar program nationally.

2.
Graduates will be able to critique a brief essay, pointing out grammatical, spelling, and punctuation errors, and offering appropriate suggestions for correction of deficiencies.

3.
Students completing the baccalaureate program will be capable of writing an acceptable journal article and having it published.

4.

5.

Form B

ASSESSMENT RECORD
FOR
<u>Undergraduate English Program (Bachelor of Arts)</u>
(Department/Program)
<u>Academic Year 1995-1996</u>
(Period Covered)

Intended Educational (Student), Research or Public Service Outcome, or Departmental Administrative Objective

NOTE: There should be one form C for each intended objective/outcome listed on form B.

1.

Students completing the baccalaureate program in English will compare very favorably in their knowledge of literature with those students completing a similar program nationally.

First

1. a. Means of Assessment & Criteria for Success:

The average score of the graduates of the baccalaureate program in English on the "Literature in English" MFAT subject test (which they will be required to take shortly before graduation) will be at or near the 50th percentile compared to national results.

---

1. a. Assessment Results:

MFAT score for this year's graduates (18) were found to be at the 37th percentile primarily due to the 23rd percentile score on "American Literature" scale.

---

1. a. Use of Results:

Course offerings in "American Literature" are being reviewed for consistency with MFAT technical description and items.

Second

1. b. Means of Assessment & Criteria for Success:

Ninety percent of the English baccalaureate program will "agree" or "strongly agree" with the statement "In the field of literature I feel as well prepared as the majority of individuals nationwide who have completed a similar degree during the past year.

---

1. b. Assessment Results:

Ninety-three percent responded "agree" or "strongly agree."

---

1. a. Use of Results:

No action required.

Form C

ASSESSMENT RECORD
FOR
Undergraduate English Program (Bachelor of Arts)
(Department/Program)
Academic Year 1995-1996
(Period Covered)

Intended Educational (Student), Research or Public Service Outcome, or Departmental Administrative Objective
NOTE: There should be one form C for each intended objective/outcome listed on form B.

2.

Graduates will be able to critique a brief draft essay, pointing out the grammatical, spelling, and punctuation errors, and offering appropriate suggestions for correction of the deficiencies.

First

2. a. Means of Assessment & Criteria for Success:

As part of a "capstone course" during the students' final semester prior to graduation, they will critique a short essay; identify grammatical, spelling, and punctuation errors; and offer suggestions for correction of the deficiencies. Eighty percent of the graduates will identify and offer suggestions for remediation of 90% of the errors in the draft essay.

2. a. Assessment Results:

Ninety-two percent of graduates identified 87% of errors. However, grammatical conventions regarding capitalization were not consistently applied.

2. a. Use of Results:

Faculty use of commonly accepted conventions regarding capitalization in upper division papers is being emphasized.

Second

b. Means of Assessment & Criteria for Success:

b. Assessment Results:

a. Use of Results:

Form C

ASSESSMENT RECORD
FOR
Undergraduate English Program (Bachelor of Arts)
(Department/Program)

Academic Year 1991996
(Period Covered)

Intended Educational (Student), Research or Public Service Outcome, or Departmental Administrative Objective

NOTE: There should be one form C for each intended objective/outcome listed on form B.

3.
Students completing the baccalaureate program will be capable of writing an acceptable journal article and having it published.

First

3. a. Means of Assessment & Criteria for Success:
All graduates of the baccalaureate program in English will prepare a journal article for submission and forward it to the department.

3. a. Assessment Results:
Articles received from all (18) graduates.

3. a. Use of Results:
No action required.

Second

3. b. Means of Assessment & Criteria for Success:
Eighty percent of those journal articles submitted will be judged acceptable for publication by a jury of English department faculty from an institution comparable to Our University.

3. b. Assessment Results:
Fifty-five percent of articles reviewed were found acceptable for publication.

3. b. Use of Results:
English 407 (advanced writing) is being modified to include journal article exercises.

Third

3. c. Means of Assessment & Criteria for Success:
Twenty percent of those articles submitted will be published in student or other publications.

3. c. Assessment Results:
Thirty percent of articles were published.

3. c. Use of Results:
No action required.

Form C